MMM8

Modern Music Masters Arctic Monkeys

Richard Bowes

Modern Music Masters – Arctic Monkeys

ISBN: 978-1-8381887-8-8
modernmusicmastersuk@gmail.com

DEDICATION

Thank you to my girls, who indulge me so patiently.

CONTENTS

Acknowledgments i

- Foreword 3
- A few words from the author 5

1 'Over there, there's friends of mine. What can I say? I've known them for a long, long time' (1986-2004) 8

2 'Anticipation has a habit to set you up for disappointment' (2005) 21

3 'I ain't got no dollar signs in my eyes. That might be a surprise, but it's true' (2006) 33

4 'Bring on the backlash!' (2006) 47

5 'We'll stick to the guns, don't care if it's marketing suicide, we won't crack or compromise' (2006-2007) 58

6 'Frightened that honesty isn't enough and it's nothing on the early stuff' (2007-2008) 77

7 'Fools on parade cavort and carry on for waiting eyes' (2009-2010) 95

8 'I took the batteries out my mysticism and put 'em in my thinking cap' (2010-2011) 113

9	'I poured my aching heart into a pop song' (2011-2013)	130
10	'Mad sounds in your ears make you get up and dance' (2013)	146
11	'Secrets I have held in my heart are harder to hide than I thought' (2013-2017)	162
12	'I just wanted to be one of The Strokes. Now look at the mess you made me make' (2017-2018)	181
13	'I wanna make a simple point about peace and love, but in a sexy way where it's not obvious' (2018-2020)	201
14	'No-one's on the streets, we moved it all online as of March' (2020-2022)	209
15	'Puncturing your bubble of relatability with your horrible new sound' (2022)	219
-	References	239
-	About the Author	246

ACKNOWLEDGMENTS

Thank you to all the following, without whom this book would not have been possible:

Thank you to Tom Boniface-Webb for entrusting me to contribute to his series, my thanks go to him for the commission and the trust he has shown in me.
Cover Design: Barry Parkinson at www.beepea.co.uk
www.discogs.com
Martin Talbot, Chief Executive, Official Charts Company
Rob Poole, Commercial Manager, Official Charts Company
The *Modern Music Masters* series is published in partnership with the UK Official Charts Company.

Books in the *Modern Music Masters* Series:

Oasis
Blur
Pulp
Manic Street Preachers
The Verve
Suede
Paul Weller – The Solo Years
Arctic Monkeys
Amy Winehouse

MMM8 – Arctic Monkeys Spotify Playlist

Available at: MMM8 – Arctic Monkeys

FOREWORD:

I would be willing to make the bold claim that the Arctic Monkeys are the most important British band of the 21st century. They are the only stadium-filling, number 1 collecting, awards' grabbing, scruffy indie band left in the UK, and the last remaining act that signals a long-gone era, where young acts like Oasis and The Verve found themselves at the top of charts. In the modern music environment, it's very important that they exist, sitting alongside Ed Sheeran and Adele as the biggest acts the UK has to offer the world.

And one of the most important things about the band is that they know how important rock 'n' roll is, and how important their place is within it. As alex turner explained at the brit awards in 2014,

> That rock 'n' roll, eh? That rock'n'roll, it just won't go away. It might hibernate from time to time, and sink back into the swamp. I think the cyclical nature of the universe in which it exists demands it adheres to some of its rules. But it's always waiting there, just around the corner. Ready to make its way back through the sludge and smash through the glass ceiling, looking better than ever. Yeah, that rock'n'roll, it seems like it's faded away sometimes, but it will never die. And there's nothing you can do about it.

Turner's band built on the existing development of fifty years' worth of working-class British culture and channeled it through the modern lens of rock 'n' roll. They took the dry wit and realism of writers like John Osborne and Alan Sillitoe and married it with the music of The Jam, The Clash and Oasis. The angry young man had become the angry young learned man, standing on the shoulders of giants to create something new, yet firmly rooted in the past. And the tunes sounded great too.

Richard Bowes' second book in the *Modern Music Masters* series brings to life one of British music's brightest lights, exploring in detail a career that spans the dizzy heights of the band's early hits, I Bet You Look Good on the Dancefloor and When the Sun Goes Down, and their incendiary first album *Whatever People Say I Am, That's What I'm Not,* and brings it right up to date, 16 years later, with their new album, *The Car*. Richard's eye for detail is second to none, and despite clocking in at 60k words, no arctic stone goes unturned in this most modern of indie-pop-rock stories.

This is of course the best place to start with a history of the arctics, but for more on the band you could explore: *Arctic Monkeys: Whatever People Say They Are... That's What They're Not* by Ben Osborne (Omnibus, 2013), or Jack Goldstein's self-published book *101 Amazing Facts About Arctic Monkeys,* from 2014.

There will be more *Modern Music Masters,* for the moment though, sit back and enjoy the eighth entry in the series, *Modern Music Masters – Arctic Monkeys.*

Tom Boniface-Webb
November 2022

A FEW WORDS FROM THE AUTHOR

If you were a fan of British guitar music in 2005, it was impossible to ignore Arctic Monkeys, even if you sneered at the name. Being an avid reader of *NME*, who by their own admission were late to the party, those two words became ubiquitous and intriguing. In what was already a strong period for the genre, a new generation of guitar bands (Franz Ferdinand, Bloc Party, Editors, Maximo Park...the list was pleasingly long) were building on the foundations left for them by The Libertines.

Although I only lived up the road, I couldn't attend the now-legendary set at Reading Festival in 2005. Nor was I able to get tickets for their live shows, as demand was just too high. However, I was among the thousands of people who bought I Bet You Look Good on The Dancefloor in October, catapulting it to the top spot. From that day to this, I've been hooked on the adventures of these four unassuming young men from High Green, Sheffield, and after finally managing to catch them at Reading Festival the following year I've been to numerous live shows times over the years.

Put simply: what a band. Clearly a cut above from the outset, no group since Oasis had made such an immediate impact on the UK, with their first two singles hitting the top of the charts followed by a generation-defining album. Not bad for a start, but once you've hit those heights, where else is there to go? Wherever they wanted.

And that's what makes them special. Rather than resting on their laurels, upon the release of *Humbug* it became clear that Arctic Monkeys were true artists who would follow their muse and if that cost them some fans, so be it. Then *AM* arrived, bringing in an entirely new generation of fans and swallowing the world. Their belated response to this mainstream, commercially successful and artistically fulfilling rock album? Release a concept album, written on piano, about a hotel on the moon. Obviously.

When they first broke through, it was apparent they weren't comfortable with the fame that comes with being pop stars, but what's interesting now is how completely in control they are. Throughout 2022, it was known that Arctic Monkeys would be releasing a new album at some point in the year, yet nobody in the music press or wider world could confidently state what it would sound like. For a band on their seventh album, that's a remarkable achievement, and their tight levels of control only add to their mystique. You may know a lot about Alex Turner, Matt Helders, Jamie Cook and Nick O'Malley, but only what they want you to know. As it should be.

Therefore, if you are expecting to read about inter-band relationships or bust-ups then prepare yourself for disappointment. I do not claim to have any special access to the band; this is written as a fan. I also don't claim that my interpretation of Turner's lyrics is definitive as, in the absence of any further insight, they are just that: my interpretation, just as you will have your own. That's the beauty of being a music fan.

Not that a lot of research wasn't required. As well as *NME.com*, which has been an excellent diary throughout their entire career (a fact for which I am eternally grateful), I must give enormous thanks to *Arctic Monkeys: Whatever People Say They Are...That's*

What They're Not by Ben Osborne (Omnibus Press, 2013).

With their artistic integrity, significant success and being the last British rock band to make an impact on the UK charts, I believe that this book is a worthwhile entry to the *Modern Music Masters* series. I hope you feel the same.

CHAPTER ONE
'Over There, There's Friends of Mine. What Can I Say? I've Known Them for a Long, Long Time' 1986–2004

Arctic Monkeys hail from the UK city of Sheffield in South Yorkshire, commonly referred to as the Steel City, an impressively fearsome nickname dating back to its prominence during the Industrial Revolution of the 19th century. Many technologies were founded in the region and the significant expansion of its traditional cutlery trade, with stainless steel and crucible steel being developed locally, was responsible for a tenfold increase in the population. As a result, Sheffield was awarded city status in 1893.

The area has a proud sporting history, with two professional football clubs vying for dominance in the city (Sheffield Wednesday and Sheffield United) in addition the city is home to the World Snooker Championship and the UK's first professional ice hockey team; the aptly named Sheffield Steelers. Elsewhere, the city is culturally familiar across the world as the setting for the movies *The Full Monty* (Cattaneo, 1997), *When Saturday Comes* (Giese, 1996), and *Four Lions* (Morris, 2010) alongside many others. And, most relevantly for the topic of this book, Sheffield's fingerprints are all over the history of UK music.

Def Leppard can stake their claim to be the first rock band to break out from the area in the late 1970s, but Sheffield is more famous as one of the breeding grounds for the genre loosely known as 'synthpop'. The Human League, Heaven 17, and Thompson Twins lead the charge for pop music with an electronic tilt that rampaged through the pop charts from 1980 onwards, ably supported by Cabaret Voltaire, albeit more of a cult concern. Indeed, such was Sheffield's importance for the burgeoning dance music scene of the era that it became the home to several historically important nightclubs, including Gatecrasher One, to which dance music fans flocked from around the globe until its destruction by fire in 2007.

Although initially more famous for other genres, Sheffield also gave birth to a handful of guitar bands who rose to prominence in the 1990s and 2000s. Britpop contenders the Longpigs' lead guitarist, Richard Hawley, was (and remains) a fiercely proud native of the city while in 2006, the five-piece band The Long Blondes set the indie charts on fire with the glam-disco Giddy Stratospheres and the accompanying album *Someone To Drive You Home*. Perhaps most famously though, and already immortalised in a separate Modern Music Masters book, three decades earlier, in 1978, a group of friends formed an alternative-pop act with the name Arabicus Pulp. After changing their name and after 16 years of toil, Pulp became of the most prominent acts of the Britpop movement, with their lead singer Jarvis Cocker elevated to national treasure status in the 21st century.

While the musical soundscapes of Sheffield were formulating, two sets of parents gave birth to young boys who would go on to further elevate Sheffield's musical heritage or, more specifically, the heritage of the suburb of High Green in the northern part of the city. On 6 January 1986, Penny and David Turner became parents to son Alex, while four months later, on 7 May, Jill and Clive Helders welcomed their second son, Matthew, into the world.

Seven years later, at a local primary school, Matthew and Alex became firm friends at the local primary school.

As is the way at primary schools across the UK, in their final year the children leaving to go to secondary school were offered the opportunity to perform at their final assembly in 1997. Backed by a couple of friends, Helders and Turner grabbed some tennis rackets and other props to use as makeshift 'instruments' and performed the quasi-title track from the second Oasis album, *(What's The Story) Morning Glory?.* Like everyone else of their age in 1997, Oasis had a hugely inspirational effect on the pair. As Turner recalled to *Pitchfork* some years later: 'With Oasis, it's just that attitude, like it's resistant against everything else that's going on in music. I don't know if you can fully understand that - it's like an impulse, innit? Especially at that age you don't rationalise, you're just like, 'That looks cool.'(i)

Given what was to come, their choices of band member were both curious and telling, with Turner opting to be Paul 'Guigsy' McGuigan, the unassuming bass player, and Helders adopting the full Liam Gallagher persona. 'He had the bucket hat on,' Turner recalled to *Pitchfork,* 'We were just standing there doing what Oasis did onstage...which was not a great deal. I don't think we got as good a reaction as the Spice Girls.'(ii)

The friendship between Helders and Turner continued throughout their time at Stocksbridge High School, which they both left in 2002 aged 16. During their time at secondary school, the pair would seek to amuse one another by creating silly band names and fantasy football teams, while Turner was also secretly writing songs. As nature dictates, these partners in crime became swallowed by wider friendship groups and became close with a youth also at Stocksbridge named Andy Nicholson (from nearby Hillsborough) and another called Jamie Cook. Cook, a guitar music fanatic and football starlet, attended the nearby Ecclesfield School and, being six months older than Turner, was in the school year above.

While Cook was a fan of Oasis and The Smiths, by the late 1990s Helders and Turner had become disciples of UK hip-hop, as the latter would explain to *Pitchfork* in 2012: 'There wasn't a lot of guitar music in my world then. I'm sure there were great bands at the time, but they just didn't make it to our little village 20 minutes outside Sheffield. We were into hip-hop in a big way, we would wear caps and shit, and our trousers definitely fit a lot less snug than they do now.'(iii)

Specifically, Turner cited London rapper Roots Manuva's 2001 album, *Run Come Save Me,* as an enormous influence: 'I think the reason why I connected to (the album) was probably because he was talking about quite mundane things with a bit of a stoned slant,' he said. 'Also, at that age, I wanted to have my own thing that other people might not have heard about. (iv) This approach would likely have seeded into Turner's own early song-writing efforts, and indeed can be heard on much of his band's material across their career.

Matt Helders was also an advocate of hip-hop, spending his formative teen years listening to UK garage and rap, both of which were the dominant forms of pop music at the turn of the century. After experimenting as a DJ at school, he turned to sampling the records of his parents, his affinity with the power of the beat developing from an early age.

After the Britpop craze fell away in the late 1990s the vacuum was filled by UK garage acts such as So Solid Crew and Artful Dodger, all of whom found significant success in the UK charts. After licking its wounds, raucous guitar music hit back in 2001, the charge led primarily by New Yorkers the Strokes and The White Stripes from Detroit. Once the doors were kicked open, a raft of high tempo rock acts followed, including Yeah Yeah Yeahs (also from the United States), The Vines (Australia) The Datsuns, and The D4, both from New Zealand, the latter act a key influence on Turner and co, with heavy chord delivery more akin to 'rock' music, as opposed to 'indie.'

Indeed, The D4 had such a formative impact on the four friends after they saw them at Sheffield's famed Leadmill in 2002, Matt Helders having a Damascene conversion at the gig, rushing out to buy their latest EP, *Ladies Man*, the following day. The wheel turned once more as the group of friends had been bitten by the bug that is 'that rock 'n' roll.' Yet the foundations for their future career had been laid the previous year, with both Turner and Cook receiving guitars on request as Christmas presents in 2001, whereby the duo set about teaching themselves (and one another) to play these divine bits of wood. So inspired were the group of friends by 'The New Rock Revolution' (as the *NME* had dubbed it) immediately after taking their GCSEs and leaving school, Turner, Helders and Nicholson decided to form a band. Cook was soon drafted in and before a note of music had even been rehearsed, he suggested a name: Arctic Monkeys.

With Nicholson opting to play bass, and Cook and Turner claiming the guitars, Matt Helders was left with only one option. According to him, drums were, 'the only thing left. When we started the band none of us played anything. We just put it together.

They all had guitars and I bought a drum kit after a bit.'(v)

Yet his dalliance with beat-based music was likely a factor in attracting the young man to the skins. After paying £200 for a kit, his friends began practicing at both Helders' parents' house and in Turner's nearby garage, with the prospective young drummer insisting upon the cymbals being placed lower down than is traditional (in the vein of Ringo Starr). The setting is to ensure his face can be seen, and he continues the positioning to this day.

Arctic Monkeys were initially a five-piece, with classmate Glyn Jones on lead vocals, each member contributing backing vocals. Jones and Turner began writing songs soon after they left school, the former having been encouraged to take centre stage. However, this would prove to be a short-lived arrangement, as the visions for the bands differed; Jones saw the band as a fun pastime whereas the rest had larger aspirations, and the contrasting perceptions of their future meant he soon departed. After trying and failing to recruit a replacement singer, the responsibility logically fell on Alex Turner's shoulders, being then chief songwriter. Reluctantly, he took on the mantle that would change his life.

The now four-piece's early sets consisted of cover versions of songs by their heroes The Strokes (amongst others) along with Turner's early compositions and rehearsals occupied much of the long summer of 2002 before Helders and Turner started two-year courses, in music technology and art respectively, at Barnsley College in the autumn. Fortuitously, the college's music tutor allowed the nascent band to use their facilities to record some of the Monkeys' cover versions, which handily counted towards Turner's coursework. Cook, meanwhile, took on the role of apprentice bathroom tiler while Nicholson started a bar job at the famous Sheffield venue The Boardwalk, eventually getting his band-mate Turner a job there too, the young man working part-time around his studies.

As time wore on, Arctic Monkeys grew in confidence and started playing gigs at The Grapes, a small venue in the city centre, with Matt Helders' parents acting as 'roadies'. Their debut gig took place on 13th June 2003, the show and subsequent gigs being invaluable in road-testing and honing their sound and enabling them to eventually find their voice as a band.

The maiden set was largely a series of covers of songs by The Strokes, The Vines, The White Stripes, The Datsuns, and The Beatles, along with a cover of Fatboy Slim's 1998 single The Rockafeller Skank. Also included were two of their own compositions which opened the set.

The setlist was:

Ravey Ravey Ravey Club
Curtains Closed
The Rockafeller Skank
Black Math
I'm Only Sleeping
Teenage Kicks
Hotel Yorba
Harmonic Generator
(Unknown Vines cover)
(Unknown Strokes cover)
(Unknown Jimi Hendrix Experience cover)

However, Alex Turner found his new role problematic. As he later revealed in an interview with *The Guardian* in 2005, he would often sing in a transatlantic drawl (aping his hero Julian Casablancas) while penning meaningless words for the sake of having something to sing. Yet the influence of Roots Manuva clawed away at his psyche, as did the everyday lyrical style of Mike Skinner (AKA The Streets), and Turner moved towards a more observational yet detached form of composition, compounded when he discovered the musings of legendary Mancunian street poet John Cooper Clarke. Despite Clarke's influence, Turner's rapid-fire delivery style owed much more to rap than it did to rock.

Distancing himself from the content allowed Turner the freedom to tackle subjects that could previously have been too close to home. As he told Dorian Lynskey in an interview with *The Guardian:* 'Even the songs that are more personal are done in that observational way because it's not as close to the bone. People can't get at me and say, 'Who's that about then?' It's a bit like you're hiding behind something. Sometimes when you write summat and you come to sing it first time in practice, instead of 'I' you put 'he,' without even thinking about it.'(vi)

At Arctic Monkeys' second gig, at The Boardwalk on 23rd October 2004, the quartet made another step forward. In attendance at the show, on the advice of Alex Turner, was local recording studio owner Alan Smyth. Recognising their potential, Smyth in turn recommended the band to Geoff Barradale, a talent scout working for the London-based management company Wildlife, who boasted Travis and Craig David amongst their clientele. After meeting with the band, Barradale signed them on the spot, a bold move which set the standard for the rapid serious of events that would soon become a hallmark of Arctic Monkeys' early career.

With Helders and Turner completing their stint at Barnsley College in the summer of 2004, the group was able to make a full-blooded commitment to their band. They set about perfecting their sound via touring, with a handful of shows outside Yorkshire, all the while shrewdly cultivating their fanbase, handing out free CDs of their demos to date.

The CDs were recorded at Alan Smyth's 2Fly Studios between late August 2003 and November 2004. The sessions, paid for by Barradale, were short and effective, the recording and mastering often taking place on the same day. Recorded 'as live', minimal tweaks were made to the recordings; normally Jamie Cook's guitars were overdubbed (as he still had a day job), as were Turner's vocals to ensure they were fully audible. In a reflection of the urgent nature of the music, the band would only record two or three takes before burning the finished article onto CDs to give out at gigs, a well-practiced means of promotion.

One fan (handily, also an associate of the band) collated the various tracks and offered free downloads to all who had the will to search for them online. Eventually compiling a full body of work, Mark 'The Sheriff' Bull christened the collective songs *Beneath the Boardwalk,* a nod to the Sheffield venue. As well as welcoming the punters who attended the original gig, making the music easily accessible would only elevate their reputation and therefore demand for their shows.

With an audience fully primed, i.e., already knowing the words to all the songs, word-of-mouth counted double for those not aware, perpetuating a growing mythology around the group. The band themselves were aware of the benefits of the approach, as Matt Helders told *Prefix Magazine* in 2005: 'The fans just used to send them (the songs) to each other, which didn't bother us because we never made those demos to make money or anything. We were giving them away free anyway - that was a better way for people to hear them. And it made the gigs better because people knew the words and came and sang along. We can't complain about it.'(vii)

Arctic Monkeys were soon dubbed 'the first MySpace band' as they became the first band of note to benefit from the internet era. File-sharing (the practice of attaining music via the internet for free) had been the bane of many acts in the early part of the 21st century, but rather than suffer from it, Arctic Monkeys were able, either by accident or by design, to use it to their advantage. It was a practice that would revolutionise the music industry. For their part, in later interviews the band would simplify the approach, merely confirming that they would just give out the CDs and let the rest take care of itself, but at the time it was seen as a visionary new way to break an artist, for which they were positioned as figureheads, their early success placed as much at the hands of the internet as at the usual practice of touring.

Indeed, members of the group would go on to claim that they weren't aware of MySpace at all, and Alex Turner later claimed that he didn't even own a computer. Now considered the first social media network to reach a global audience, MySpace was initially launched as an online data storage and soon transitioned into a to a social networking site, where like-minded people could meet online and share content (such as music) with their new friends.

The site quickly grew an audience, primarily of teenagers (always the most tech-savvy), and by 2003 became a pop-culture point of reference, the precursor to Facebook and Twitter. The file-sharing was, in its simplest terms, a modern version of the mixtape. It did, however, build a relationship between the artist and the fan, curating a new level of devotion with the end user garnering a feeling of affection from the individualized touch.

In 2005, amidst their rise, the media were eager to put Arctic Monkeys' success down to the internet, without ever considering the notion that it may have been due to the quality of the songs. Although burgeoning, the practice of posting music online wasn't new; The Libertines had previously posted much of their work online for free and David Bowie, ever the sage, is credited as the first mainstream artist to release music online, his single Telling Lies on the internet before a physical release in 1997. Other artists followed the practice with little fanfare or success, the cream rising to the top. Or put more basically, they didn't have the songs. Arctic Monkeys did.

Of the 18 tracks that made up *Beneath the Boardwalk*, 11 would eventually be released on the first few official releases from the band. Yet it's remarkable how similar a lot of the songs are to the finished versions: A Certain Romance, Dancing Shoes, Fake Tales Of San Francisco, Mardy Bum, Scummy Man (which became When the Sun Goes Down) and I Bet You Look Good on The Dancefloor are all much the same as the versions that ended up on the band's debut album, barring some improvements in production. Bigger Boys and Stolen Sweethearts and Still Take You Home have some slight lyrical tweaks, while the latter and Stickin' to The Floor are much rawer and heavier. Riot Van has more of a brusquer feel and underwent a lyrical overhaul after this recording, while Cigarette Smoke (later Cigarette Smoker Fiona) is darker content-wise in comparison to what it would become.

Of those that didn't make the grade, four share a common theme: girls. The snarling Choo Choo has a funky bass motif running through it accompanied by a wired guitar, its lyric a metaphor for either male dominance in a relationship or perhaps in a more carnal setting. While the influence of The Strokes purveys throughout the collection, Knock A Door Run is the most obvious example; a mini-opus, akin to those that would follow, about the games of attraction.

The groovy Wavin' Bye to The Train or The Bus has an intense verse but a deft, innocently romantic chorus which would become a trademark of their early era. On The Run from The MI5 is a primal little rocker, not dissimilar to You Probably Couldn't See for The Lights but You Were Staring Straight At Me (and may have been an earlier version) written from the perspective of a 'crack dealing crook', but with a flat chorus beneath the band, even at that early stage.

Space Invaders seems to be about drug abuse, but Turner's ambiguous writing style had already begun. It's a rollicking wig-out nonetheless, while the forgettable Curtains Closed is apparently a conversation about the frustrations of normality within a relationship. Lastly, Ravey Ravey Ravey Club (live) is raucous punk, the recording adding to the effect in sounding like a 1970s bootleg. As the title suggests, it's about nightlife and the power of 'magic beans.' Being demos, the sound is brittle and frailer, but the songs are still impressively familiar. The foundations of their first album are undoubtedly here, if not most of the structure in question. All that was needed was a lick of paint.

CHAPTER TWO
'Anticipation Has a Habit to Set You Up for Disappointment' (2005)

Moving into 2005, Arctic Monkeys' touring schedule kicked into a high gear. Largely freed from the constraints of education and employment (although Jamie Cook kept working full-time for a spell), the foursome toured the UK throughout the year, solidifying both their reputation and their fanbase. The touring saw their musicianship improve: Matt Helders was fast becoming the most spontaneous drummer of his generation; Andy Nicholson was a solid but free-wheeling bass outlet while Cook was at home playing either power chords or plucking strings to suit whatever the song required.

Alex Turner, no slouch on guitar himself, had established a singing voice (distinguished by delivery in his native Sheffield accent) while his song craft combined wry cynicism, impersonal observations, or first-person musings with ease. Understandably, they were starting to get noticed. Among the first to comment was BBC South Yorkshire, noting that they 'blew away headliner Tom Vek, not that anyone is really bothered about him. To all intents and purposes, this is a Monkeys headline show and they well and truly steal it,'(viii) when reviewing their show at The Room in February.

Although there were reservations about how exactly the band would make them money, record labels were scrabbling for their signature, but A&R people were banned from their gigs, the group resentful of the unnecessary advice that was coming their way. They had done things their way and, with positive results thus far, there seemed little need to alter that tactic until the right offer came along.

At their first *NME* interview and photoshoot (for the magazine's *Radar* column, spotlighting new bands), journalist Rick Martin would note that, even though it was merely a rehearsal, Alex Turner spent time tuning his guitar to ensure the sound was perfect and avoid any possible negative press.

So confident were the group and the team around them, they headed into the studio to re-record two tracks and subsequently released them as a limited-edition debut EP (3000 copies in total, split equally between vinyl and CD) on their own label: *Bang Bang*. With no barcode, the record was ineligible for chart placing and, although widespread practice for dance acts to self-release their music, indie bands doing the same was a rarity. It did, however, ensure the recordings were up to a standard that could get them radio play.

EP 1:

Five Minutes with Arctic Monkeys
Released: 30th May 2005; UK Chart Position: N/A;
Label: Bang Bang Recordings
Track Listing: Fake Tales Of San Francisco; From the Ritz to the Rubble
Producer: Mike Crossey

Once again, when re-recorded for their debut album, the two tracks were left virtually unamended. Fake Tales Of San Francisco later underwent one lyrical change ('the band aren't very good' became the more scathing 'the band were fucking wank'), but its ska-tinged verse and call-and-respond chorus (of sorts) remained. Their musical dexterity was already apparent; the second verse subtly adds more jangly guitar sounds to signify the song's progression while Matt Helders spices up his drums further with superb cymbal work as the second half of the song explodes into a riotous outpouring of frustration.

The frustration and withering cynicism were aimed at the other participants in the music scene. Perhaps conscious of their decision to incorporate their roots proudly, Turner cuts the wannabe rock stars down to size in a scathing three minutes, reminding them that, 'you're not from New York City, you're from Rotherham,' and to 'get off the bandwagon and put down the handbook.'

It contains numerous killer lyrics, the best being: 'But his bird said it's amazing so all that's left is the proof that love's not only blind but deaf.' Turner's capacity to tinker with expressions and phrases was already of a high quality, the influence of John Cooper Clarke shining through.

The second track would also feature on the debut album: From the Ritz to The Rubble contains verses that Turner delivers at a machine-gun pace, regaling the story of the night before with a tinge of regret while his bandmates aren't found wanting, clattering in and out when required. 'Last night what we talked about made so much sense, but now the haze has ascended it don't make no sense anymore,' is a universal recognition when hungover, Turner finessing his social commentary skills. The EP sold out on pre-orders alone, allaying any fears that fans who already owned the downloads would not be interested in a physical version.

Meanwhile, the momentum and hype continued. A gig at Camden's legendary Dublin Castle became infamous, as the crowd in attendance sang every word back to the band but also because Steve

Lamacq, Radio 1 DJ, and bastion of new indie music, wasn't allowed in as the show was beyond capacity.

The anecdote was another useful story to add to the flourishing legend. Allowing demand for the band's signature to reach unprecedented levels, therefore giving them carte blanche to choose the label they would sign to, was a shrewd move by Geoff Barradale. Having met with and been impressed by the passion of Laurence Bell, head of Domino Recording Company, they chose to sign with his label.

Although an independent label, Domino had a strong roster of clients including Glaswegian art-rockers Franz Ferdinand, who in 2004 had two top 10 hit singles (Take Me Out and Matinée) a Mercury-winning top 3 album (their eponymous debut) and an Ivor Novello award to their name. Such an ascent, managed with integrity and dignity while giving the band full artistic control, appealed to the Monkeys' team and so they signed with Bell's label.

With the record deal in the bag, Arctic Monkeys stepped up their touring in earnest, with a headline set at the 1,000-capacity Leadmill in their hometown selling out in seconds. They set about recording their debut album, allocating production responsibilities to James Ford (from the band Simian Mobile Disco), and choosing to once more record at 2Fly Studios, with further sessions taking place at The Chapel Studio in Lincolnshire.

The group was starting to attract the attention of the mainstream press, with Dave Simpson from *The Guardian*, in attendance at their show at the Birdwell Club in Barnsley, noting that the group 'have brought a modern twist to a traditional route,' and 'if they can remain this sharp and unspoilt, Arctic Monkeys will be the sound of next year.'(ix) Meanwhile the *NME*'s Mark Beaumont decided at a Birmingham show that, 'Arctic Monkeys will soon be transcending such bottom rung polemic – they've the sass, suss and swagger to carve us a new route through modern pop, the urch button in hand and a snivelling anti scene sneer in their lip.'(x)

The summer tour culminated with a mid-afternoon slot at the Reading & Leeds Festival in late August. The first show, at Reading, swiftly became the stuff of legend. The Carling Stage, a modest tent designed to spotlight unsigned or up-and-coming bands, saw twice its capacity attempt to muscle in and catch a view of this burgeoning phenomenon. Walking on stage, Alex Turner acknowledged the event and the ravenous crowd with a single missive: 'Don't believe the hype, Reading. They haven't hyped us up enough.'

The set, only eight songs, began with Fake Tales Of San Francisco as the tent erupted and didn't subside, with When the Sun Goes Down and I Bet You Look Good on The Dancefloor bawled back to the band at deafening volume. The show in Leeds (close to their hometown), was equally rapturously received. Before the festival, Arctic Monkeys were a 'must-see' band of the weekend. Afterwards, the sets became 'were you there' moments, much like the Sex Pistols at Manchester's Lesser Free Trade Hall, with Conor McNicholas, *NME* editor, citing it as the moment his magazine became redundant.

In 2021, McNicholas appeared on the podcast *22 Grand Pod* claiming that he realised during that gig (which he had attended intending to scope Arctic Monkeys' suitability for the *NME* tour in the New Year), with a huge portion of the crowd was singing every word, that *NME's* position as tastemaker and news outlet was over. Without giving any publicity to Arctic Monkeys they had built up a fan base by going directly to their audience through the internet, ensuring that printed news outlets would become quaint in the age of instant information.

Their maiden festival sets were followed by the band's first TV appearance, on the contemporary music show *Later...with Jools Holland,* which allowed the nation to cast judgement on this group making waves. The physical appearance of the boys added to the myth; in casual attire, the camera close-ups revealing their spotty teenage faces, the band ripped through a storming version of forthcoming single I Bet You Look Good on The Dancefloor with confidence, Matt Helders amending his backing line, 'you're dynamite,' in tribute to fellow guest Miss Dynamite. Once work was complete on the album, the group embarked on another sold-out tour at circa 1,000-capacity venues.

Their first show (upgraded from the Mean Fiddler to the Astoria in London) saw hundreds of fans, hoping to get tickets outside the venue, crestfallen with the 1,200-capacity venue sold out. With Alex Turner in a Little Flames T-shirt (a band with whom they had become friends), Arctic Monkeys took to the stage and tore straight into I Bet You Look on The Dancefloor. Turner demonstrated his crowd-pleasing nous by allowing the crowd to sing the opening words of the final chorus, a trick he would employ hereafter.

Due to their reticence in interviews (or even to engage in them), the band had garnered a slight reputation as surly and unresponsive, but when playing live, it was a different story. Turner engaged with the crowd frequently, often performing lyrics (miming having a drink, etc) when he was able to. During Perhaps Vampires Is a Bit Strong But... Turner (without guitar), plodded around the stage and expressed with his arms (in the style of a rapper) before picking up his instrument for the second half of the song, his onstage chat cheekily irreverent and endearing ('Is this where the celebs come and watch us then, London? Oh, you're all celebs to me,').

The excessive touring meant their set was by now honed to perfection. Owing to the stop-start nature of their music, some mistakes could be expected but the group were watertight in their delivery, almost telepathic at points. Turner would, mid-song, comment to the crowd but, regardless of the length of time of his speech, the band would crash back into the song faultlessly, displaying awe-inspiring levels of control and musical discipline.

Betty Clark, reporting for *The Guardian*, witnessed the show and made lofty, but valid, comparisons: 'Adolescent alchemists and reckless romantics, Arctic Monkeys have fused the best of the two most iconic bands of the past decade. Oasis's gift for anthemic melodies meets polished-up Libertines' rhythms under Turner's taunting sneer, but it's the brutal, bruised lyrics, iced with northern sensibilities, which set Arctic Monkeys apart, although their barely defined features make them look as if they've just been dragged, feet first, out of the womb.'(xi). All this before a note of music had been available in the shops.

But Arctic Monkeys couldn't deny the music industry any longer and their official debut single, released to coincide with the UK tour, was finally unleashed on the world in October 2005. To the surprise of everyone who hadn't been paying attention, it went straight in at number 1 on the UK Singles Chart.

Single 1:

I Bet You Look Good on The Dancefloor
Released: 17th October 2005; UK Chart Position: 1;
Label: Domino; Album: *Whatever People Say I Am, That's What I'm Not*
B-Sides: Bigger Boys and Stolen Sweethearts; Chun-Li's Spinning Bird Kick
Producer: Jim Abbiss

UK Singles Chart – Top 10 – 23rd October 2005:

1. **I Bet You Look Good on The Dancefloor – Arctic Monkeys**
2. Push The Button – Sugababes
3. I Wanna Hold You – McFly
4. Tripping – Robbie Williams
5. Don't Cha – Pussycat Dolls ft Busta Rhymes
6. Gold Digger – Kanye West FT Jamie Foxx
7. Baby Goodbye – Friday Hill
8. Bad Day – Daniel Powter
9. We Be Burnin' – Sean Paul
10. Song For Lovers – Liberty X

In comparison to much of their early work, I Bet You Look Good on The Dancefloor is lyrically basic, but as an introduction to Turner's wordsmithery, it works well. Although a song about desire, the internal monologue from the narrator suggests conflict and resentment that he's unable to control his desire: 'I wish you'd stop ignoring me because you're sending me to despair, without a sound yeah you're calling me, and I don't think it's very fair'. He doesn't want to be so primal and obvious as to be driven by lust but knows he has little choice.

The person, who we know is called Rio (from Duran Duran's song of the same name), is a glorious mystery ('I don't know what you're looking for,') but the narrator knows what it isn't: 'there ain't no love, no Montagues or Capulets.' Turner would later confirm its simplicity, namely gazing at one person when you are with someone else. Much to the confusion of analysts, the 1984 in question wasn't a reference to George Orwell's dystopian classic, but to an electro-pop group fronted by Jon McClure, a friend of the band.

The singer wasn't keen on his lyrics, however. Speaking to Dorian Lynskey from *The Guardian,* he revealed that he felt it was, 'a bit shit. The words are rubbish. I scraped the bottom of the barrel. It could be a big song like. But I'd hate to just be known for that song because it's a bit...crap.'(xii) It was instantly clear that a special lyricist was emerging; few other songwriters of the era would merge Shakespeare and club life so succinctly and perfectly to illustrate a point.

Even if the lyrics weren't up to Turner's lofty standards, musically it was the sound of something new and exciting. As a mission statement, it was brave to open with a guitar solo that wrenches the instrument to sound like industrial machinery, but it immediately locks the listener in. The rhythm section, despite the rigidity of the song, flourishes with Nicholson's rolling bass holding its own against Helders' sparky drumming.

The accompanying B-sides didn't carry the same level of energy, but then few songs do. Bigger Boys and Stolen Sweethearts, a tale of the universal heterosexual teenage experience, slips between narrative viewpoints ('You said you wasn't sad to her go, I was only pretending you know,') and is therefore immediately relatable to anyone who was ever that age (and gender), while the deft guitar during the verse is a more controlled version of Pete Doherty and Carl Barat's singular guitar chaos. Meanwhile, Chun-Li's Spinning Bird Kick, a reference to a character from the *Street Fighter* computer game (as confirmed by the opening sneer of 'show us your special move,') is a crunching, strutting instrumental, one of the few in the band's career.

Although reluctant to engage in the media game, there was nowhere to hide for Arctic Monkeys from this point on. Even the video for the single was unassuming; the band, shot in a studio in the style of *The Old Grey Whistle Test,* just got on with the job, barring a brief introduction from Alex Turner: 'We're Arctic Monkeys, this is I Bet You Look Good on The Dancefloor. Don't believe the hype.' The video came in handy for their maiden appearance on British staple *Top of The Pops*; when informed they would be required to mime, the group refused and so the video was used instead.

Despite Turner's warning, the hype was, for once, justified. Although pop acts would often hit number 1 in the chart with their debut singles (explicitly in the early 00s with the rise of *The X-Factor),* for an indie or rock band to do so was unprecedented. Ordinarily, a band would take at least one album before breaking into the mainstream, and, while Franz Ferdinand hit heights early in their career, this was on a different scale. Even Coldplay, revered from the start, were yet to have a number 1 single, despite releasing their third album and becoming a stadium band earlier in 2005.

Indeed, although a crop of guitar bands was

making waves (Kaiser Chiefs, Bloc Party, Hard-Fi), very few had troubled the top 5, apart from Razorlight with their non-album single Somewhere Else in April 2005. When it came to British guitar bands only Oasis, more than 10 years into their career, were troubling the upper echelons of the Singles Chart. This was both a game-changer and a metaphorical gauntlet being thrown down. Or it could have just been because Arctic Monkeys were better than everyone else.

Desperate to find a reason for the band's meteoric rise, the mainstream media was caught off-guard and latched on to the by-now tired idea that the band's success was due to the strange practice of sharing songs via the internet. This simplistic version of events (with various tabloid headlines simply stating 'Arctic Monkeys reach No 1 thanks to the internet') demonstrated a lack of understanding that file-sharing was a new form of marketing they were unfamiliar with, ignoring the fact that the release in question was an exceptionally good song.

Aware of criticism regarding this and the hype around the band generally, Alex Turner did his best to play things down in an interview with XFM: 'We didn't do anything to help make it get to number one, if anything we went the other way. We didn't put loads of different formats out or anything, we just released it. It's great for music and that, but nah, we never thought, 'We've got to top that with another Number One.' We just want to try and make the record as good and interesting as it can be.'(xiii) Elsewhere in the same interview, Turner revealed he saw his writing as a combination of the styles of Mike Skinner and Jarvis Cocker.

The breathless pace of events wasn't just confined to the UK. After a short European tour,

Arctic Monkeys performed a few dates in the United States. Due to demand, a gig at The Mercury Lounge in New York City was upgraded to the Bowery Ballroom with one David Bowie, apparently retired but with his finger perennially on the pulse, rumoured to be in attendance. An extraordinarily successful year, the first of many, ended with Alex Turner topping *NME*'s annual Cool List before the Christmas break, a break the band would surely need. If things had been hard to comprehend up to this point, it was about to get even crazier.

CHAPTER THREE
'I Ain't Got No Dollar Signs in My Eyes. That Might Be a Surprise, But It's True' (2006)

The turn of the year saw the band lift a second single from their forthcoming debut album. When the Sun Goes Down, previously known as Scummy or Scummy Man, was a narrative tale about prostitution on the working-class streets of an unnamed British town, the 'man' is either a pimp or a regular 'client', who treats the protagonist badly. The narrator is concerned with the plight of the girl, the last line of the song pleading: 'I hope you're not involved at all.'

Musically the song has an odd structure, the opening bars consisting only of Turner's singing and a sequence of clean electric chords, but turns on a sixpence as the line, 'he's a scumbag don't you know,' heralds a crunch of metallic guitars, a driving riff, and faster pace. Turner's vocal delivery in the second half of the song is notably more outraged and aggressive.

He would later confirm that When the Sun Goes Down was inspired by observing questionable characters and young women near and around the industrial estates in which the band's studio in Neepsend, Sheffield was located. In addition, the line, 'he told Roxanne to put on her red light,' is a nod to The Police's 1978 track Roxanne, also about prostitution. Overall, a brave choice for a single.

Single 2:

When the Sun Goes Down
Released: 16th January 2006; UK Chart Position: 1;

Label: Domino; Album: *Whatever People Say I Am, That's What I'm Not*
B-Sides: Settle for a Draw; Stickin' to the Floor; 7
Producer: Jim Abbiss

<u>UK Singles Chart – Top 10 – 23rd January 2006:</u>

1. **When the Sun Goes Down – Arctic Monkeys**
2. Nasty Girl – Notorious BIG/Diddy/Nelly
3. All Time Love – Will Young
4. Check On It – Beyonce ft Slim Thug
5. That's My Goal – Shayne Ward
6. JCB Song – Nizlopi
7. I'll Be Ready - Sunblock
8. Say Say Say (Waiting 4 U) – Hi-Tack
9. Break The Night with Colour – Richard Ashcroft
10. Eddie's Song – Son of Dork

Given the context of the hype around the band, with the debut album only weeks away, it's perhaps not a surprise now that the single went to number 1. Yet viewed from a distance, if it was unheard of for a new indie bank to hit the top spot once (which could have been written off as a fluke), then for a group of 19/20-year-olds to do so at the second attempt is the stuff of fantasy. Yes, all the reviews for the band's live shows and the forthcoming album were uniformly supersonic, but the average consumer would likely save themselves some money and wait for the album's release. The fans and the people couldn't get enough of Arctic Monkeys.

The video, directed by Paul Fraser, was a

confusing watch on initial viewing. It featured a cast of characters including British actor Stephen Graham (most recognisable from Guy Ritchie's crime caper *Snatch* and *Gangs Of New York,* directed by Martin Scorsese) as the formerly titular character who, even amongst the fast edits, can be seen to fulfil the role supremely, and Lauren Socha, later to find fame in the Channel 4 show *Misfits*. A sequence of events, including interactions from both characters with a magician, is open to interpretation but the viewer is left with no doubt as to the tone.

A few months later, a short film (*Scummy Man*) from which the video was taken was released on DVD by Domino. It becomes clear that Socha's character (Nina) is a drug addict with little choice but to prostitute herself for money, bringing her into the orbit of both Graham's Scummy Man and the magician. The film pulls no punches, showing violence towards men and women, drug abuse, and the desperation of the characters involved. It makes for a harrowing watch. Matt Helders appears briefly as a musician who Nina attempts to coerce, while the rest of the band appears very briefly towards the end.

As grim as Part One of the film is, Part Two (*Just Another Day*) offers hope, recounting the same story but from the perspective of a man who takes a shine to Nina and tries to offer her protection, the young girl reminding him of his daughter who passed away some time before. The film ends with the man and his wife finding Nina at her lowest ebb and offering her solace, thereby proposing that hope can be found in the darkest of times. It's not an immediate association with Arctic Monkeys, but this alignment with other forms of media, namely films, would continue throughout their career.

When the Sun Goes Down was backed with

three B-sides across various formats. Stickin' to the Floor is a slight thing, at under 90 seconds, with Turner expressing disgust at the types of young men who are perpetually hostile and intimidating ('Not one of you has got an ounce of style in ya'). Settle for a Draw is a standard rocker, still recognisably the band but less explosive than many other songs of the era, the subject compromise in a relationship. 7 has a bit more vigour, with 90 seconds of lyrics before a short workout for the band which then resolves itself. To celebrate the success of their second number 1, Arctic Monkeys played a gig at The Leadmill.

The success of When the Sun Goes Down (even with the *Top of the Pops* embargo maintained) was more of a surprise given that their 'target audience', namely their enthusiastic fanbase, owned the song long before its official release, either from the file-sharing or because the album leaked on to the internet over the festive period. Consequently, the album, given the title of *Whatever People Say I Am, That's What I'm Not,* was brought forward in the release calendar by one week.

Album 1:

Whatever People Say I Am, That's What I'm Not
Released: 23rd January 2006; UK Chart Position: 1; Label: Domino
Track Listing: The View from The Afternoon; I Bet You Look Good on The Dancefloor; Fake Tales Of San Francisco; Dancing Shoes; You Probably Couldn't See for the Lights but You Were Staring Straight At Me; Still Take You Home; Riot Van; Red Light Indicates Doors Are Secure; Mardy Bum; Perhaps Vampires Is a Bit Strong But...; When the Sun Goes Down; From the Ritz to the Rubble; A

Certain Romance
Producer: Jim Abbiss
All songs written by Alex Turner except Still Take You Home written by Alex Turner and Jamie Cook

Laurence Bell had introduced the band to James Ford with a view to his producing the album. However, the production duties eventually fell to Jim Abbiss, a former musician who had worked with guitar and electronic bands in the early 1980s before training as a producer under Owen Morris, producer of the first three Oasis albums (as well as The Verve's *A Northern Soul*). After this, Abbiss took part in countless remix sessions for the acid house movement of the late 1980s/early 1990s, before eventually becoming chief engineer at Maison Rouge Studios in London.

During his tenure, Abbiss worked with Steve Hillage and Nellee Hooper, as well as James Lavelle on his UNKLE recordings, including his remix of Bittersweet Symphony, The Verve's classic single from 1997. Ford had started recording four tracks for *Whatever People Say I Am, That's What I'm Not* alongside Mike Crossey (the band's first producer) but the overall production responsibilities were allocated to Abbiss. Ford's involvement with Arctic Monkeys would continue far beyond these sessions and would encompass more than just production.

Mardy Bum (recorded at 2Fly) aside, the entirety of the album was recorded at Chapel Studios in South Thoresby, Lincolnshire over 15 days during the autumn of 2005. Abbiss was initially brought in simply to remix the *Beneath the Boardwalk* tracks until the band intervened, feeling they would be short-changing fans by asking them to pay for something they already owned. Abbiss set about recording the whole group together, along with Ford, with the guitars miked up and the two guitar amps put into separate sound booths.

Unconventionally, the bass was taken out and set up in a corridor, meaning the band could play live but with everything recorded separately. The original idea was to play the songs live without any vocals (with Alex Turner overdubbing them later), but this proposal initially confused Turner as he had become accustomed to playing and singing live. After so many months of performing, it was a learning curve for the foursome to play the songs at a slower pace but necessary to ensure everything was distinct.

The album's title was taken from Karel Reisz's 1960 film adaptation of Alan Sillitoe's classic 1958 novel *Saturday Night and Sunday Morning*, starring Albert Finney in one of his first screen roles. Finney plays the role of Arthur Seaton, a young man in working-class surroundings in the north of England. Seaton works in a factory and only finds excitement in his town through drinking, having an affair with a married woman, and annoying the locals. Trapped within his area, he feels he's better than those around him and resents his situation (hence the line) but is powerless to do anything about it; post-war, people rarely left their hometowns to venture into a new life.

The film ends with Seaton preparing to settle down with a local girl, defiant that he will do better than his parents but still staying in Nottingham. It struck a chord with Turner and, given the themes of the album, clearly influenced him more than pilfering one line suggested. More cinematic associations would follow.

The frontman wasn't the first British musician to be inspired by *Saturday Night and*

Sunday Morning. Another famous line from the film ('I believe you. Thousands wouldn't,') was used in The Beatles' 1965 comedy caper *Help!* directed by Richard Lester. In addition, The Stranglers used the title for a live album in 1993, and the run-out groove on the B-side of vinyl copies of The Smiths' 1986 masterpiece *The Queen Is Dead* features the line, 'them was rotten days', also taken from the film.

Indeed, Morrissey claimed *Saturday Night and Sunday Morning* was a firm favourite of his, and another line ('why don't you ever take me where's it lively and there's people?') is likely to have inspired a lyric from There Is a Light That Never Goes Out. Finally, Arthur Seaton was mentioned in the song Where Are They Now? from The Kinks' 1973 album *Preservation Act. 1.*

The cover of *Whatever People Say I Am, That's What I'm Not* featured a friend of the band (Chris McClure) in a profile shot. McClure, the frontman of Sheffield band The Violet May and the brother of John, was part of the Monkeys' circle of friends. According to the band, they had given McClure, his friend, and one of his cousins £70 to spend on a night out in Liverpool. After fulfilling his task, McClure presented himself, cigarette in hand, for a photo shoot in the small hours of the next morning. The interior artwork for the album had a corresponding photo as a representation of each song.

All of which added to the theme. Broadly speaking, *Whatever People Say I Am, That's What I'm Not* is a concept album centred around 24 hours in the life of a young man in Sheffield, although it could have been any city or town in the UK (barring a couple of specific references), which is why it mattered, and made the impact it did, in parallel with the perfect alchemy of the band. The delivery of the music, urgent and watertight as it was, was unlike anything else in the indie scene (being noticeably heavier and more American-influenced) and fluctuated to fit the vibe of the songs, sounding bigger than Turner's mundane musings while complementing them wonderfully.

The View from The Afternoon sets the scene poetically; while not stated in the song itself, the title informs the listener of the perspective of the song and the timeframe of the album. The song starts explosively, a cacophony of rock music, before settling into a jerky, angular rhythm for the verse, scanning beautifully with an opening line ('Anticipation has a habit to set you up for disappointment,') which works on two levels: both within the narrative and, more widely, a nod to the hype the band had been embroiled in up to this point.

As an opening statement, it sits alongside the Stone Roses ('I don't have to sell my soul, he's already in me,') and Oasis ('I live my life in the city, there's no easy way out,'). Yet the cynicism is overwhelmed by the excitement of a night out ('Tonight there'll be some love,'), which continues throughout the remainder of the verse. Then, from nowhere, the song turns on a sixpence with the 'bridge' (Arctic Monkeys rarely follow traditional song structures), Turner's delivery of 'she won't be surprised,' declaring their intentions: presume nothing.

It was one of the last songs written for the album, and it shows. Heavier, more confident than much (though not all) of what follows, it's full of little flourishes such as Matt Helders' cymbal work between lines in the riff. Although the line, 'when she's pressed the star after she's pressed unlock,' may date it (a feature of Nokia phones. Remember them?), the notion of 'verse and chapter sat in her inbox and all that it says is that you've drank a lot,' was both prescient and timeless, such is the dangerous combination of alcohol and mobile technology.

I Bet You Look Good on The Dancefloor sustains the momentum musically, narratively still looking ahead to the night to come, while the ruminations of Fake Tales Of San Francisco seem to take place in the first pub. Dancing Shoes starts as a groovy, danceable call-to-arms before evolving into a monstrous rock beast, all clashing cymbals and crunching chords, the delivery (by all the band) of, 'the only reason that you came,' undoing the party mood with menace.

Although delivered in the second-person, Turner's inner thoughts perfectly capture the insecurity and doubt of the would-be peacocks: 'Don't act like it's not happening,' as if the first instinct to play it cool ever works, 'instead you'll just do the same as they all do and hope for the best', as the shyness pervades.

You Probably Couldn't See for the Lights but You Were Staring Straight At Me, on which Matt Helders dictates everything including the pace and delivery of the first line, picks up the story. The object of our hero's desire has attracted other potential suitors, making the anxiety worsen, but a conversation has started: 'I'm talking gibberish, tip of the tongue but I can't deliver it properly,'. The pace of the song is relentless, akin to The Strokes in chord structure but much faster, a breathless rattle through our understanding of guitar music.

Rattling just as intensely, Still Take You Home fluctuates its pace at will, with the protagonist seemingly having a conversation with the recent object of desire, only to find there is little substance beneath the style ('I can't see through your fake tan...what do you know? You know nothing!') but faces the common dilemma of being unable to control his carnal desires, hence the title. Our hero is disappointed in himself as he knows he's no better than those he has been sneering at.

The first half of *Whatever People Say I Am, That's What I'm Not* is a collection of thunderstorms that leave the listener gasping for breath, not least by being subjected to Turner's rapid-fire vocal delivery. The band knows this and allows us some respite. Ironically a song with a more confrontationally intriguing title, Riot Van is a melancholic, kitchen-sink, cobbled street track. Gentle and frail, it shows another side to the band's style, a weariness or exhausted cynicism put over sparser music, proof that these lads were no one-trick ponies. Playing with expectations, the action in the narrative (of the police arriving) is action-packed in comparison, detailing that part of the night where everyone has had too much to drink.

The taxi arrives and takes our group of friends home at the end of the night on the bopping, ska-flecked Red Light Indicates Doors Are Secured which, unlike many of the other songs, contains snippets of the conversations that would take place in such a scenario. The lines, 'Well, how funny were that sketch earlier up near that taxi rank? Oh no, you would have missed it, think it were when you went to the bank,' may appear basic by its direct rhyming, but not only does it recall the previous song, it is the sort of off-hand comment that contributes to the realism. The Lathums, among many other bands, were listening carefully.

The next day arrives in the form of Mardy Bum, or the great single that never was. Moving away from a quasi-ska style into a version of heavy skiffle, the lyrics cover a sheepish soul trying to reason with their partner about their tardiness and dishevelled demeanour on the morning after the night before. As close as we get to a ballad on the first album, it's a quiet, disconsolate but accepting view of the flaws and frustrations in a relationship. A singalong moment during their gigs and a fan favourite even before its release.

A sidestep from the apparent narrative arrives next, in the form of Perhaps Vampires Is A Bit Strong But...musically not dissimilar to what has gone before but moodier and more intense. The first signpost towards the next step in Arctic Monkeys' career, from the mid-section onwards the band rock out and sound like they are having fun, even indulging in a drum solo. Alex Turner uses his voice well, adjusting the inflections when it suits him and, as live appearances would demonstrate, this was not accidental but well-planned.

A diatribe against those people around them who were 'certain we'll fail', Turner confronts them directly, informing them that, 'I don't want your advice or your praise, or to move in the ways you do, and I never will.' This speaks to the less vocal (in interviews) aspect of the group; they may have appeared shy but not when singing their opinion while being clever enough to nullify any negative aspects that may come their way. The vampires in question are almost certainly predatory music industry people.

It's a push, but to crowbar it into the narrative; it could be taking place on Sunday afternoon as the group is engaging in some hungover rehearsals which, when followed by When the Sun Goes Down and its observations of the activities that took place near their rehearsal space in Neepsend, retains the linear plot. From the Ritz to the Rubble follows this sequence, our hero recalling a tale of a close shave when trying to get into the club the night before.

The album ends with a summary of events and, more broadly, the general situation most young people find themselves in if they stay in their hometown. An epic piece, A Certain Romance sees the hero considering his surroundings where 'there's only music so that there's new ringtones,' and a general vibe that the humdrum life they are living is all becoming too soul crushing.

It's the classic dilemma that many before Turner have had; departing a town and friendships for your own sake, while both leaving a part of yourself there and taking some of it with you as you venture onwards. The band clatter in before a solo strum of a guitar, present throughout the main body of the song (representing the determination and the resigned reflection in turn) before one last go at battering their instruments, which conveys well the intention of facing the future with one look back.

The final verse before the maelstrom ('over there, there's friends of mine. What can I say? I've known them for a long, long time, and yeah, they might overstep the line, but you just cannot get angry in the same way,'), speaks to anyone who has been embarrassed by their friends but is protective of them at the same time. They are idiots, but they're your idiots and, when one returns home, they don't seem to have changed, for better or for worse.

Whatever People Say I Am, That's What I'm Not crams a lot into its 41-minute runtime, an emotional rollercoaster even over a decade and a half on. The references which now date it were so pertinent at the time that young people across the UK felt it spoke to them, and that it represented their lives, in a way that other bands couldn't.

Despite swiftly becoming the voice of a generation, Turner played down all expectations and simplified his song writing process in an interview with *The Irish Times*: 'They're just observations. It makes sense to write about what I see around me and what I know. It's a bit like hip-hop in that sense. You get the words, you make sure they make sense, you get the words to rhyme and away you go.'(xviii) It sounds obvious, but the difference between a genius and a mortal is that they make their art look obvious.

While A Certain Romance and Perhaps Vampires Is a Bit Strong But...indulge themselves with outros that ensure they exceed four minutes, every other song is watertight and brief, few exceeding the 3-minute mark, yet its genius is that it feels like more, so intense is the experience. It may be the perfect album.

The reviews were overwhelmingly positive. The *NME* awarded it 10/10 and were effervescent in their praise, observing that, 'even if you've been fortunate enough to live with these tracks over the last year or so, they still sound more vital, more likely to make you form your own band than anything else out there,'(xiv) while *Rolling Stone* was confident that, 'the reality nearly meets the hype.'(xv) *The Guardian* was also pleased, Alexis Petridis noting that the album 'defies you not to join in the general excitement,'(xvi) although *Pitchfork* was an outlier, witheringly (and inaccurately) declaring that Arctic Monkeys were, 'the same sort of meat'n'potatoes guitar rock that has dominated the UK since the emergence of the Strokes, if not Oasis,'. (xvii)

Not that the reviews were ever going to

matter. *Whatever People Say I Am, That's What I'm Not* sold just under 120,000 copies on the day of release, nearly doubling HMV's first-day prediction. By the end of the week, it was selling 82 copies a minute and eventually reached a figure of 363,735, making it the fastest-selling debut album of all time in the UK, smashing the record held by Hear'Say (a product of the UK talent show *Popstars*), held since 2001. Which of course meant it shot to number 1 on the Albums Chart.

UK Albums Chart – Top 10 – 29th January 2006:

1. ***Whatever People Say I Am, That's What I'm Not* – Arctic Monkeys**
2. *Keys To the World* – Richard Ashcroft
3. *Stars Of CCTV* – Hard-Fi
4. *The Back Room* – Editors
5. *From Daniel with Love* – Daniel O'Donnell
6. *Back To Bedlam* – James Blunt
7. *Keep On* – Will Young
8. *Veneer* – Jose Gonzalez
9. *Inside In/Inside Out* – The Kooks
10. *Employment* – Kaiser Chiefs

The album also hit the top spot in Ireland and Australia as well as making the top 10 in New Zealand, Japan, the Netherlands, Finland, and Belgium. No small feat, and it later became the second-fastest debut indie album in US history.

CHAPTER FOUR
'Bring on the Backlash!' (2006)

Despite the astonishing success of *Whatever People Say I Am, That's What I'm Not,* Arctic Monkeys were already moving on from its song writing style. Appearing on Steve Lamacq's show on BBC 6Music the week before the album's release, Alex Turner revealed: 'It's a very different life already. There's no way we'd be able to write that sort of stuff again.' Showing wisdom beyond his years, he continued; 'But that's always the case, innit? I think, as long as you know that and don't try and pretend to be that anymore, then it's fine. We've got quite a lot of new songs since the record and none of them are about them sort of things.'

As was fast becoming apparent, Arctic Monkeys were always on the move, and no sooner had the album been released than they were on the road again, as part of the *NME* Awards tour. Initially proposed as first on the bill, for security reasons they were promoted to second to Newcastle art-rockers Maximo Park, with We Are Scientists and Mystery Jets completing the line-up. However, it soon became clear that the Sheffield lads were the main attraction (with all due respect to Maximo Park) and they swapped places with the headliners at the Sheffield show.

Toying with the crowd, at their request they played the opening chords of Love Machine (which they had recently covered for BBC Radio 1's *Live Lounge*) before launching into A Certain Romance. The recorded version of Love Machine featured Turner and Helders playfully alternating both vocals and gender perspectives, depending on what the delivery of the lyrics over the melody required.

During the *NME* tour, Alex Turner revealed that a new song, Do Me A Favour, was 'the further adventures of the girl in Mardy Bum – my ex.'(xix) The band had also been performing another new song not on their debut (Leave Before the Lights Come On) for several months. Meanwhile, the tour took place at the same time as the 2006 Brit Awards, which saw Arctic Monkeys pick up the British Breakthrough prize. Recording an acceptance video from their tour bus, the four band members sat on either side of We Are Scientists' Keith Murray, who gave a generic speech, much to the amusement of the actual recipients.

They did attend the *NME* Awards the following week and picked up a hat-trick of Best Track, Best New Band, and Best British Band, a feat matched only by Oasis and The Strokes. On collection of their third award, having used up all his best quips for the first two, Turner proposed the not unreasonable question, 'In all honesty, who else were going to be Best British band? You know what I mean - you can't write about something that much and then tell us we're not Best British Band.' They had been portrayed as shy lads, but they also had an undercurrent of steel and belief which served their predecessors well.

After another European jaunt, a full American tour beckoned in March 2006. The conditions had been set for their arrival, as *Whatever People Say I Am, That's What I'm Not* entered the Billboard charts at an impressive number 24, with an appearance on *Saturday Night Live* solidifying their presence in the United States. An eye-catching appearance at South by Southwest followed, hyped in a similar vein as their maiden performance at Reading & Leeds Festival, before they supported their childhood heroes Oasis in Toronto.

It was fair to call Arctic Monkeys a phenomenon by the spring of 2006, and Domino was keen to capitalise on the success of the album by lifting another single from it, widely anticipated to be The View from The Afternoon. True to their contrary form, Arctic Monkeys had other ideas. Although the opening track from the debut was on the EP, they somehow managed to find time to head back into the studio during their packed schedule, and they held sessions at Motor Museum in Liverpool and London's Konk Studios, finishing four new tracks that would form the basis of a new EP.

EP 2:

Who the Fuck Are Arctic Monkeys?
Released: 24th April 2006; UK Chart Position: N/A; Label: Domino
Track Listing: The View from The Afternoon; Cigarette Smoker Fiona; Despair in the Departure Lounge; No Buses; Who the Fuck Are Arctic Monkeys?
Producers: Jim Abbiss (Track 1); Mike Crossey (Tracks 2-5)

Cigarette Smoker Fiona was a reworked version of the similarly titled track on *Beneath the Boardwalk*, albeit with completely revised lyrics about a female, possibly a rich socialite, who is hosting a party that gets out of control, but still delivered with gnarly garage tones. The jaunty No Buses, based around Turner's guitar with the rest of the band popping in and out, covers matters of the heart, with the title referring to a common British expression ('you wait for ages for a bus and then three come along at once,') using the metaphor to refer to his new-found popularity with the opposite sex (the burden of being a rock star).

But the meat of the EP lies in the other two tracks. Despair in the Departure Lounge was unquestionably the most moving song by the band to date, even if calling it a 'band' song lacks credulity (apart from a snippet of backing vocals). With just an electric guitar, a handful of chords, and his voice, Turner composed a heart-rending ode to an ex-lover, using the mask of a character but surely delivering his thoughts, looking within himself after a breakup.

Continuing his unerring eye for British comedy institutions (following on from the Frank Spencer reference, the hapless character from *Only Mothers Do 'Ave 'Em* on You Probably Couldn't See for the Lights but You Were Staring Straight at Me), Del and Rodney Trotter (referred to the other way round to suit the melody) from *Only Fools and Horses* are mentioned, specifically, the scene where Del falls through the bar, often referred to as the funniest UK television moment of all time. Yet the sparseness of the production is loneliness as music.

The EP's title track was Arctic Monkeys at their most direct. There is little ambiguity as to what the lyrics mean: a tale of how stardom can lead to disappointment ('your heroes aren't what they seem when you've been where we've been,'), their steadfast refusal to play a manipulated record industry game ('don't care if it's marketing suicide, we won't crack or compromise,') and an astute line which introduces the closing sequence ('Bring on the backlash,'), after some threats of violence. Similar in structure to A Certain Romance but darker in tone with a skanking beat and, of all things, a key change, the song once again nullified the inevitable bad press the band would likely soon receive, through the disconcerting British habit of building them up only to knock them down.

Indeed, by this point Alex Turner was consciously playing games with the press, confirming in an interview with *Nuts* that, 'we ruffle feathers pretty well. I think, when you're in a position to do some feather-ruffling, it's not always a bad thing. I don't even know why we do it – we just like being fucking little naughty boys sometimes.'(xx)

Although not a single, The View from The Afternoon did come with a video, directed by W.I.Z., who had videos for Oasis, Stereophonics, and Black Rebel Motorcycle Club to his name. The short film featured a young man playing a drum kit in a housing estate in Sheffield, alternating between night and day, and includes several characters, such as a girl, a gang of young men, and a man with a baseball bat (at his wit's end with the incessant drumming) and takes place over several hours. The video pauses midway through (at the same point as the song) and reveals that, despite having bandaged them in preparation, his hands are bleeding. The same shot shows that the young man has a tattoo of three intersecting circles on his wrist, a nod to Led Zeppelin drummer John Bonham, who had adopted the sigil.

As an EP, *Who the Fuck Are Arctic Monkeys?* was ineligible for both the UK Singles (too long) and UK Albums Chart (too short) and so didn't chart on either. An accompanying DVD of *Scummy Man/Just Another Day* was released in April, which finally explained the frantic video for When the Sun Goes Down. The *NME* was impressed, declaring that; 'all songs as amazing as we've come to expect,'(xxi) although *Drowned in Sound* felt that, aside from the opener, 'the four tracks that follow vary from the boring to the dire,' and, perhaps unknowingly, called the title track 'self-referential postmodernism.'(xxii)

Undeterred, Alex Turner referred to the EP as 'a mission statement, if you like. We want to do things our way, and people think it's arrogance, so it's inevitable some people will get tired of us.'(xxiii) The irony being, of course, that by releasing something that was ineligible for the charts and featured swearing in its title, they could be seen to be engineering a flop, almost taunting the industry.

Arctic Monkeys were becoming so big the conversation was even reaching the upper echelons of UK society. When asked who his favourite band were (as part of a continual attempt to display the government as 'down with the kids'), Chancellor of the Exchequer and Prime Minister-in-waiting Gordon Brown namechecked the Sheffield foursome. He was later forced to admit he couldn't name any of their songs but was able to comment that the group was 'very loud.'

Sadly, it seemed the momentum was taking its toll on the band members too. On the eve of their US tour, the band announced that Andy Nicholson wouldn't be joining them. The official statement read: 'Owing to fatigue following an intensive period of touring, Andy Nicholson shall be taking a rest and will not be accompanying Arctic Monkeys on their forthcoming tour of North America. Nick O'Malley shall be standing in for Andy on the tour which begins in Vancouver on May 27th. We all wish Andy a speedy recovery.'

The breakneck and ongoing speed of events affecting the band members shouldn't have been a surprise; they had been working incredibly hard for two years with an increasingly busy itinerary. Nick O'Malley (also from High Green) a long-standing friend and jamming partner with the band, and previously a member of The Dodgems, was a logical and easy choice to step into Nicholson's shoes temporarily. To bed O'Malley in, the group played a small show at the Old Blue Last in East London, where they referred to him as a 'friend of the band.' Ironically, O'Malley wasn't 100% fit either, yet still managed to play much of the American tour while nursing a broken arm.

The American dates went well but when they returned to the UK there was a surprising development. In another official statement, Arctic Monkeys announced: 'We are sad to tell everyone that Andy is no longer with the band. Nick O'Malley, who stood in for Andy while he was absent from the recent tour of North America, shall carry on playing bass for the remaining shows this summer. We have been mates with Andy for a long time and have been through some amazing things together that no one can take away. We wish Andy the very best.'

A few weeks later, speaking to Zane Lowe backstage at the Oxygen Festival in Ireland, Alex Turner put Nicholson's departure down to touring: 'We were in Lisbon at the end of the European thing and he decided he didn't want to come to America. And that was cool, and then, I don't know, I guess we found ourselves in this situation by the end of the American tour.' Turner went on to sympathise with his now ex-bandmate: 'I mean, a lot happens, it's not just like three weeks in a normal thing, it's three weeks with your head all over the place. I mean, it's a really difficult thing to explain, I don't think anyone will really understand this except us three and

Andy.'(xxiv)

In a later interview, Turner elaborated: 'We sorta found ourselves in a situation where we wanted to move forward. It weren't like us wanting to carry on like this as punishment for him wanting to opt out.' Jamie Cook, meanwhile, was defiant in the face of potential criticism: 'Everyone might say we're wankers and we shit on him, but they don't know. We know, Andy knows and that's all that really matters.'(xxv)

The entire situation was clouded in mystery, as was perhaps to be expected from a group who kept their cards so close to their chest. However, when appearing on *The Michael Anthony Show* podcast in 2019, Andy Nicholson provided some more details on his version of events: 'It was kind of a sticky one really. I remember we'd just finished the UK tour which finished at Brixton Academy. If I'd known what was going to happen, I would have made that the last gig I ever did.'

'The next day, we (were) going on a European Tour, and I had to stop off and deal with some family stuff off at home and after that tour were meant to go and record, and then go on tour in America. 'I can't really do that right now; I've got some stuff I need to take care of.' Sometimes, you gotta prioritise what's important at that moment as well. You can always look back and think, 'maybe I should have done that as well...they came back off that America tour and they said, 'we're gonna keep Nick.'

'I had no idea. I got to the pub, no one's there. The manager's assistant is sat outside the pub in his car and said, 'we're not meeting here.' (We) jumped in the car and up to Jeff's office. We just started talking (and then) they said that. Once they said it, I thought, 'Right, well that's a decision made.' Al

(Turner) did the speaking. Jamie did a little bit. I'm not saying that all was like 'Oh yes, let's do it! Let's pull this plug,' or anyone enjoyed any of it.'

'I remember all that happening in that room. I just thought, 'How am I going to deal with this?' It was probably one of the very few soul-destroying moments (in my life). I remember being in that room and, once they said it and I just thought, 'OK let me just try and keep a bit solid about this,' so I stood up, shook all three of their hands, said 'good luck' then I walked outside and threw my jumper on the floor.'

A new permanent line-up established, Arctic Monkeys covered their summer with numerous European festival appearances, including at Eurokeenes in Belfort, France, where the band was so impressive that Julian Casablancas, a hero to the band, conceded the Arctic Monkeys were too tough an act to follow. Sustaining the momentum, and to reintroduce themselves to the UK Singles Chart after seven months, the group released a brand new, one-off single.

Single 3:

Leave Before the Lights Come On
Released: 14th August 2006; UK Chart Position: 4; Label: Domino; Album: N/A
B-Sides: Put Your Dukes Up John (The Little Flames cover); Baby I'm Yours (Barbara Lewis cover)
Producer: Jim Abbiss

UK Singles Chart – Top 10 - 20th August 2006:

1. Hips Don't Lie – Shakira
2. Ridin' – Chamillionaire ft Krayzie Bone

3. Love Don't Let Me Go (Walking Away) – David Guetta Vs The Egg
4. **Leave Before the Lights Come On – Arctic Monkeys**
5. Everytime We Touch – Cascada
6. Me & U – Cassie
7. Ain't No Other Man – Christina Aguilera
8. You Give Me Something – James Morrison
9. Unfaithful – Rihanna
10. Dancing In the Dark – Micky Modelle V Jessy

The song was recorded as part of the sessions for the first album but, presumably because of the sheer volume of strong songs available, didn't make the final cut. Matt Helders' persistent snares drive the track, matched by the guitars which convey the feeling of regret and remorse of the subject matter, around a one-night stand. The lyric, 'How can you wake up with someone you don't love and not feel slightly phased by it?' perhaps unintentionally revealed Alex Turner to be a romantic, rather than a cad.

The single was backed by two covers. Put Your Dukes Up John by Liverpool act The Little Flames (featuring one Miles Kane) was, while being slightly faster, an otherwise faithful version. In acknowledgement of their broadening influences, the remaining track was a version of Barbara Lewis' lavish ballad Baby I'm Yours, originally released in 1965, with a guest appearance from Oisin Leech from the 747s who supplied the instrumentation, rather than Helders, Cook, and O'Malley/Nicholson. The latter's last recorded contribution to Arctic Monkeys' pantheon, it hit number 4 in the UK Singles Chart.

The accompanying video, directed by John Hardwick and filmed in the Cultural Industries

Quarter in Sheffield, starred Kate Ashton (best known for the zom-rom-com *Shaun of The Dead*) and Paddy Considine, the lead in Shane Meadows' thriller *Dead Man's Shoes*. The narrative of the film sees Considine's character rescue Ashton from a suicide attempt, with a shoe falling from a nearby building catching his attention. After taking Ashfield's character to a nearby café she becomes enamoured with Considine, but he refuses her advances. Rejected, Ashton returns to the rooftop and drops another shoe as Matt Helders (wearing a Bang Bang T-shirt) walks by, implying the events are cyclical.

CHAPTER FIVE
'We'll Stick to the Guns, Don't Care If It's Marketing Suicide, We Won't Crack or Compromise' (2006-2007)

After a busy summer, Arctic Monkeys played their biggest UK show to date: second on the bill at the Reading & Leeds festival (beneath sci-fi rockers Muse), just 12 months after the slot in the Carling Tent. Perhaps more than any other, this was a clear barometer of the strides made by the band over one year. No nerves were apparent as they ripped through an hour-set with vigour, which may to them have become tired. Turner, in particular, seemed comfortable as a frontman with many eyes upon him. As rapturous as the reception they received in Reading (broadcast live on TV), it paled in comparison to the reaction of the Yorkshire crowd. Heart-warmingly, while in Leeds, the band reunited with Andy Nicholson backstage, with the *NME* reporting that he was seen shaking Nick O'Malley's hand.

The setlist:

I Bet You Look Good on The Dancefloor
Still Take You Home
You Probably Couldn't See for the Lights but You Were Staring Straight At Me
Leave Before the Lights Come On
Cigarette Smoker Fiona
Perhaps Vampires Is A Bit Strong But…
Dancing Shoes
The View from The Afternoon

Bigger Boys and Stolen Sweethearts
From The Ritz to The Rubble
Fake Tales Of San Francisco
Mardy Bum
When The Sun Goes Down
A Certain Romance

And the accolades kept coming. A few days after Reading & Leeds, the Mercury Music Award ceremony took place in London, with *Whatever People Say I Am, That's What I'm Not* the comfortable favourite, despite fierce competition. Arctic Monkeys picked up the award, and Turner, Helders, and Cook stepped up to the podium to receive it from ceremony host Jools Holland. Referring to another nominee, fellow Sheffielder Richard Hawley (with his album *Coles Corner*), Alex Turner, with shorter hair than at Reading & Leeds, quipped: 'quick, someone call 999, Richard Hawley's been robbed.'

Speaking to the press after the ceremony, the trio was in a spiky mood. One journalist asked the band how they were feeling, to which Jamie sneered in response: 'That's a reet original question.' After being asked why they didn't perform at the ceremony, the guitarist replied, 'Muse didn't perform. Ring them up and ask them why they didn't fucking perform.' Another journalist asked if Andy Nicholson would get a share of the prize cheque and Helders responded: 'no, it's going to a charity that he'll agree with,' to which Turner added, cryptically and under his breath, 'And I'm certain he will.'

The next question, 'what does it mean to you to win this award?' was immediately cut down by Cook: 'we've had that one, don't ask it.' Another journalist enquired as to why the band had stepped away from dealing with the media, to which Cook sneered once again, 'because of these shit questions.'

'We're doing a social experiment to see if we have to or not,' Helders elaborated. After being asked a third time how it felt to win the award, Cook gave the reporter short shrift: 'ask another fucking question!' The whole situation did little to help the band's reputation as surly and awkward young men, not that they seemed to care (nor should they have done). But perhaps aware of the likely negative press, a statement on behalf of the band was later released:

'We had a fantastic night and we're really chuffed with winning the award. It was unexpected but it means a lot to us as the competition was from other musicians we really respect. We strongly believe in the ethos of the Nationwide Mercury Prize in that it is about the music and not everything else that goes with it and we are therefore really flattered by the decision.

'Regarding the £20,000 cheque, we are going to donate it to a worthy charity which we would prefer to keep private. We have discussed it with Andy, who played an equal part in the making of the album, and he is happy with our choice. As for the near future, we are really looking forward to taking a break to continue writing our new album.'

Later in September, in an interview with the *NME*, Alex Turner revealed further details about the second album: 'We'll do a few gigs in December, but we're going to start rehearsing on Friday for the new record and we're going in next month to do some recording.' He also revealed how many songs they had in place: 'About 13 or 14 songs, but it's in different states. It might be just an idea, it might be something I've done with someone played on acoustics and some of them we all know it already, all the arrangements and shit like that.' In the same interview, Matt Helders revealed that a January release date was possible, if unlikely: 'It will probably be a bit later, but you never know. I think from our point of view we could have it ready for then.'(xxvi)

While locked in the studio, Arctic Monkeys picked up more award nominations, including a Grammy for Best Alternative Music Album and a *Q* Award for Best Album, the latter of which they won. Continuing his irreverent acceptance style, Turner, referring to the recently reformed 'man-band' Take That (*Q* Idol winners), said: 'I'm not old enough to know a lot...but even I know Take That were bollocks!' Meanwhile, to cap an incredible year, the band announced a huge outdoor show at Lancashire Country Cricket Club for summer 2007, with a second date added after the first sold out in three minutes.

Returning to both Motor Museum Studios in Liverpool and London's Konk Studios, the band set about recording their second album in the autumn of 2006. In addition, they also used Eastcote Studios, also in the capital. Having worked with James Ford (by now dubbed 'the Fifth Monkey') since their debut, he was assigned full production duties for their sophomore effort, even providing additional guitar on selected tracks.

In January 2007, Alex Turner gave the *NME* an update on the new album: 'In terms of sound, a lot of the ones we've done so far are a bit full-on. A bit like From the Ritz to The Rubble, The View from The Afternoon, that sort of thing. We've tried to get proper rhythms – it seems like in rock there's a lot of boring rhythms. We've tried to experiment – that's a bit of a dangerous word, but we've tried to push on with that. We'd be in soundchecks and it would be, 'Fucking hell, what's that?' so we'd record it on a phone. We've ended up with breaks almost. I've always been into beats, we were into that before we were into The Strokes.'(xxviii)

The first album was still making tremors, however, and the band picked up Best British Album and Best British Act at the 2007 Brit Awards. True to form, they weren't in attendance but recorded two acceptance speeches, both of which were formal and consciously unexciting. More interesting was their attire; for British Album they were dressed as The Village People, while in the speech for Best British Act they were adorned as the four adventurers from *The Wizard of Oz* (a slight hint for the forthcoming album), both examples of their surreal sense of humour. They did grace the *NME* awards with their presence the following week, picking up Best Album and Best DVD (for *Scummy Man*) along the way.

Rumours swirled during the early part of the year that Arctic Monkeys would be making their debut appearance at Glastonbury Festival (2006 having been a fallow year), with organiser Michael Eavis letting the news slip. When asked directly, Matt Helders told the *NME:* 'Er, if Michael Eavis said it, well we must be then. I can't really confirm anything. Nothing gets announced until March, and though stuff leaks out, they can always change it!'(xxviii) They were, however, able to announce details of their new album in February, formally titled *Favourite Worst Nightmare.* In addition, they announced a stellar line-up for the Lancashire Cricket Ground gigs in the form of Amy Winehouse, The Coral, and Supergrass.

Although the album was announced for an April release, impatient fans wouldn't have to wait long for new material. In mid-February, the foursome played a series of secret gigs in smaller towns across the UK. As well as Sheffield, there were small shows in Leicester, Morecambe, Middlesbrough, and

Warrington, where they debuted new songs, This House Is a Circus, Balaclava, D Is for Dangerous, Fluorescent Adolescent, Do Me A Favour, Brianstorm and What If You Were Right the First Time? Tickets for the shows were only released on the day of the performance, with queues outside the venues leaving many fans disappointed. Following the shows, they announced a larger UK tour for the spring. With everything in place, Arctic Monkeys released their fourth official single in March 2007.

Single 4:

Brianstorm
Released: 16th April 2007; UK Chart Position: 2;
Label: Domino; Album: *Favourite Worst Nightmare*
B-Sides: If You Found This It's Probably Too Late; Temptation Greets You Like Your Naughty Friend; What If You Were Right the First Time?
Producers: James Ford and Mike Crossey
All songs written by Alex Turner except Temptation Greets You Like Your Naughty Friend written by Alex Turner and Dizzee Rascal

Manifestly drawing a line under their previous work, the single release for Brianstorm opened not with the song itself but instead with If You Found This It's Probably Too Late. It was a curious move until the lyrics were revealed: 'Not sure we're ready but probably rough, frightened that honesty isn't enough and it's nothing on the early stuff,' once again pre-empting criticism while also scathing of the practices of the music industry.

The track opens with gentle strings as if to goad the listener that Arctic Monkeys, like so many bands before them, have softened or taken the easy option in 'expanding' their sound, but 90 seconds later they've comprehensively wrong-footed anyone who thought they'd be so obvious. After the strings, the song bursts into life amid a screech of garage guitars and breathless vocal delivery, reassuring fans that the band they loved was still in there.

As a return statement, Brianstorm is perfect. Opening with thundering (naturally) drums and surf-rock tremolo guitars approaching like, fittingly, an oncoming storm, the instruments ratchet up the excitement as this new era explodes into life. If possible, Matt Helders (who only undertook drum lessons after the first album had been released), pounds harder, faster, and even more relentlessly than before, while the cast iron chords batter from the other side. As if to show off, the band's trick of stopping and starting rigidly is repeated several times, which also works in presenting them as sturdier and tougher.

The Brian in question was a real person. While in Tokyo the previous year a guy (wearing a T-shirt and tie combination) burst into their dressing room with a business card in hand. He regaled the group with stories of his experience before disappearing as quickly as he came in, which inspired Turner to imagine how their potential suitor experienced life as a sequence of misadventures.

Track three, Temptation Greets You Like Your Naughty Friend, is a collaboration with London rapper Dizzee Rascal and accordingly has a hip-hop beat to accommodate his mid-song rap. The title ensures the subject matter needs no explanation and the line, 'I don't ever want to hate you so don't show me your bed,' continues Turner's theme of attempting to keep love and lust apart.

What If You Were Right the First Time? features a moody vocal from the singer with strangled guitars and yet more marauding drumming, more frayed than their previous work. The lyrics pointed toward the theme of the forthcoming album: 'Betwixt and between the fantasy dream and the fear,' is almost Shakespearean, with the remainder of the song conveying the dark suspicion that one's partner is cheating on them, having previously had their fears allayed.

The video, simplistic in comparison to previous efforts, featured the band playing on a sparse sepia set interspersed with clips of female dancers, stock footage of old medical education programmes, and snippets of words from the lyrics. It was shot on the same day as the Brit Awards, though likely not the reason they didn't attend the ceremony.

<u>UK Singles Chart – Top 10 – 22nd April 2007:</u>

1. Beautiful Liar – Beyonce & Shakira
2. **Brianstorm – Arctic Monkeys**
3. Give It to Me – Timbaland/Furtado/Timberlake
4. Girlfriend – Avril Lavigne
5. Stop Me – Mark Ronson ft D Merriweather
6. Because Of You – Ne-Yo
7. I Wanna Have Your Babies – Natasha Bedingfield
8. Away From Here – The Enemy
9. (I'm Gonna Be) 500 Miles – Proclaimers/B Potter/A Pipkin
10. The Sweet Escape – Gwen Stefani ft Akon

Sadly, the single just fell short of the top spot, peaking at number 2. One could suggest that while the novelty factor of the band had worn off, they were still going to be a chart force to be reckoned with, a fact proven by the appearance of Temptation Greets You Like Your Naughty Friend hitting number 77 in the Singles Chart through downloads alone.

In 2006, the Official Singles Chart incorporated downloads into their charting system, which allowed tracks to chart one week before their physical release and were recorded alongside their digital release. Gnarls Barkley's Crazy was, infamously, the first track to hit the number 1 spot on downloads alone (Black Eyed Peas' Pump It being the first to enter the Top 40), but the following year the UK Singles Chart fully integrated downloads by allowing them to chart regardless of whether they had a physical release.

This move, the biggest change in chart history, completely changed the Singles Chart. Where previous tracks had to be a specific and chosen release from the album, the barriers to inclusion were gone. Shortly after the rules changed, Snow Patrol's Chasing Cars returned to the Top 10 despite having been released eight months earlier and others followed suit, meaning what was previously a 'singles' chart was now, more accurately, a 'song' chart.

For better or for worse, this meant that everything was fair game and, over a decade and a half on, the Christmas charts (for example) are entirely predictable and clogged up with festive favourites, based as they are on streams (replacing downloads as the digital option of choice).

On the other hand, the democratisation of the charts has meant that, through public campaigns, older tracks can find themselves back in the higher echelons of the charts despite no re-release. The most infamous examples (in response to the continued success of *The X Factor*'s conveyor belt of anodyne pop) were Rage Against the Machine, the unlikely holders of a coveted Christmas number 1 in 2009 with Killing in The Name Of. More recently, Jarvis Cocker's 2006 single Running the World hurtled back to the top 3 as a response to the Conservative Party winning the 2019 General Election.

The *NME* hailed Brianstorm as 'a rampant return'(xxix) and appetites were suitably whetted for the album, which followed a week later. In a long interview with the same magazine, Alex Turner was more forthcoming about the band, and indeed himself, than he had previously been. When asked about their determination to play the music industry game their way, the lead singer responded, 'That probably came from Cookie. We just didn't want to look silly, really. It gets so blown out of proportion. We wouldn't do some stuff that was daft, but then it becomes, 'these boys just say no!' and that's bad because then everybody tip-ties around you.'

Referring to the subject matter of the album Turner provided some insight into certain tracks: 'There's a lot of temptation in the album. Do is For Dangerous is like a fantasy of having done the deed and you need to escape the surrounding you've been led to, but it's more just a fantasy about it, knowing you haven't actually done it. And The Bad Thing is these three things that happened, meeting three lasses on separate occasions and it all ended up in there.'

The closing track 505 was described as 'the first proper love song we've done,' and Do Me Favour was a 'goodbye, really, and about me being a bit of a knob. Perhaps I were craving to experience something else and looking back and feeling like you were a bit of a knobhead, just in how you perhaps treated that person. It's just describing a goodbye.'(xxx)

<u>Album 2:</u>

Favourite Worst Nightmare
Released: 18th April 2007; UK Chart Position: 1; Label: Domino
Track Listing: Brianstorm; Teddy Picker; D is for Dangerous; Balaclava; Fluorescent Adolescent; Only Ones Who Know; Do Me a Favour; This House Is a Circus; If You Were There, Beware; The Bad Thing; Old Yellow Bricks; 505
Producers: James Ford and Mike Crossey
All songs written by Alex Turner except Balaclava written by Alex Turner and Nick O'Malley; Fluorescent Adolescent written by Alex Turner and Johanna Bennett; and Old Yellow Bricks written by Alex Turner and Jon McClure

Although Turner was becoming more honest and direct with the ideas behind his lyrics, that was only half the story. If the first album was Turner looking out at the world in front of him, *Favourite Worst Nightmare* finds the young man in a more introspective mood. Thematically the album is about dream (and nightmare) states, hypothetical scenarios, and deep fantasies set to a creepy carnival backdrop.

Brianstorm was a musing on the antics of a real person while Teddy Picker, a type of arcade machine where the player fishes for teddy bears with a metal claw, is about the celebrity life. The arcade machine is designed to keep one's attention but somehow always evades its real target, and Turner translates this to people who are desperate for fame when there is nothing really to attain by doing so. So desperate that they 'provoke the punchline before they have told the joke', falling over themselves to be heard, they shouldn't 'be surprised when you get bent over', i.e., taken advantage of. The song drives along and turns on a sixpence like The View from The Afternoon before it, but subtly, the prodding, nosey riff sustaining the pace.

As confirmed in the *NME* interview, the rowdy, bass-driven D is for Dangerous is a sexual fantasy, as the protagonist 'thinks first a parallel universe could be the perfect scene,' with the dance music beat (complete with 'drop') that the band had mentioned previously. It also namechecks the album title, and we should all be relieved that it was chosen over some of the other apparent contenders: *Lesbian Wednesdays, Gary Barlow*, or *Gordon Brown*, the latter surely a reference to their namecheck by the incoming Prime Minister.

More carnal thoughts appeared during Balaclava, as 'he' hides behind the titular balaclava, a 'flawless heist of all time,' as a metaphor for sexual antics; 'now the shaggers perform and the daggers are drawn, who's the crooks in this crime?' Musically it's a hurdy-gurdy with circus guitar licks, the heaviness in line with the first album. Cook, Turner, and O'Malley go up and down their respective frets quickly at first, before somehow getting even faster, stopping to allow Matt Helders to indulge in some cowbell-tapping.

Fluorescent Adolescent is a rarity in Arctic Monkeys' canon in being a co-write (although not the only one on the album) credited to Turner and Johanna Bennett. Bennett, Turner's ex-girlfriend, assisted in the lyrics while the pair were on holiday, although the lyrics weren't inspired by their own relationship. The song describes a sexually unsatisfied woman who not only 'likes her gentlemen not to be gentle,' but also dreams of her past life, recalling a 'slag, the best you've ever had, is just a memory,' and was a spiritual cousin of Mardy Bum. Some astonishing wordplay and wonderful rhyming couplets are aided by superlative drumming from Helders, who keeps his skin work interesting despite a more traditional beat. At exactly three minutes, it's the perfect pop song and it came as no surprise when it was chosen as the next single.

More poignancy pervades on Only Ones Who Know, a dreamy ballad complete with crooning from Turner. A slow, 1950s-esque romantic track, it betrays its composer as a boy out of time and a precursor to the melancholy songs on *Submarine.* Notable for consisting of sparse instrumentation (the rest of the band apparently absent), it tells a tale of two lovers, a young man who 'couldn't wait to get away,' and a less-engaged female who 'told a million people that she'd stay in touch.' A slice of seaside, end-of-pier melodrama which excellently demonstrates Turner's cinematic way of writing, the song sliding away as if taken by the tide.

Fittingly for a group who rattled through their career at a blistering pace to this point, *Favourite Worst Nightmare* sees Arctic Monkeys evolving over its 38 minutes. The first half of the album follows a similar structure to their debut's relentless pace, with some minor tweaks and tucks to the formula. In contrast, the second set of songs ventures towards a different space, given room to breathe once Turner and co have the freneticism out of their system.

Do Me A Favour is a brooding opus, initially all tom-toms and wiry guitar, as the elements that make up the song are added sequentially before Matt Helders takes it by the scruff of the neck. As confirmed by its author, the song is about the break-up of a relationship and the storied emotions that are involved during the act itself, the narrator 'forcing a smile and waving goodbye', but culminating in anger, as 'perhaps 'fuck off' might be too kind.' A journey that packs so much into its 3.27 runtime.

The element of motion is continued on If You Were There, Beware but differs in clattering immediately rather than building up gradually. The carnival motif emerges once more, both through the riff and the haunted, ethereal middle eight in which Turner, with his voice, effected through a megaphone, decries 'a circle of witches, ambitiously vicious they are,' (a reference to *Macbeth*?). As a famous pop star, the people close to Turner were regarded as fair game by the tabloid press and, indeed, ex-girlfriends had been targeted by the press or the 'serpent soul pinchers.' The line, 'can't you sense she was never meant to fill column inches? Ain't you had enough? What you're trying to dig up isn't there to be dug,' seems to support this hypothesis.

The two songs above sandwich This House Is a Circus (berserk as fuck), a fuzzy, bolstering song about a situation or event, possibly a party, in which things have gone awry and people are under some sort of influence ('their memories are pretend and the last thing that they want is for the feeling to end,') while 'scaling the corridors for maidens in the maze,' ultimately deciding that 'now that we're here, we may as well go too far.' The album's cover, a nondescript grey house in Liverpool on the outside but with psychedelic, colourful artwork in the interior, could be the visual representation of The House itself.

There's little ambiguity as to the content of The Bad Thing (the remaining co-write), written with Jon McClure (brother of the first album's cover shot, Chris), otherwise known as the titular Reverend from Reverend and The Makers. Comparatively straightforward, it's a tale of attempted temptation by a woman to a man and the group's simplest song thus far, in both execution and lyrics. Its place on the album is open to question, given that stronger songs were available.

Perhaps finally an explanation of their unusual attire at the Brit Awards, the bouncing Old Yellow Bricks pays direct tribute to *The Wizard of Oz* (no explanation for the Village People choice was forthcoming, however) in its title and the payoff line: 'Dorothy was right though.' The song is about fantasies of misguided escapism ('Houdini, love you don't know what you're running away from,') before eventually surmising that there is no place like home atop a four-to-the-floor beat and viola-tinged keys.

The album's closer, 505, opens with an organ that replicates a sequence from Ennio Morricone's score for *The Good, the Bad, and the Ugly* to rubber-stamp the cinematic feel of the album. It slowly, almost imperceptibly, pulses into life with special guest Miles Kane, from their mates The Little Flames, joining Alex Turner in sequence before it explodes into a maelstrom of motorik guitar rock.

Possibly his most personal lyrics to date, it's another break-up song but one which reveals heart-wrenching insights into his broken soul: 'I'd probably still adore you with your hands around my neck,' being the standout along with the kicker that brings about the cacophony ('I crumble completely when you cry,'). A chorus of only two chords and a staple of the band's live set, generally placed towards the end, it's an explosive end to the album which proved that Arctic Monkeys were in it for the long haul.

For want of a better word, *Favourite Worst Nightmare* has a more mature sound than *Whatever People Say I Am, That's What I'm Not,* despite its chief creator's age being just 21. Alex Turner takes time over his vocals and develops his voice while Matt Helders shows that he can master more traditional drumming but ultimately serves the song regardless. Nick O'Malley slots in seamlessly, offering some ESG-esque basslines while Jamie Cook adds gusto or dexterity appropriately.

The unsettling carnival atmospherics would go on to influence countless guitar acts, including The Horrors, The Blinders, and The Rascals (Miles Kane's second band). Meanwhile, the ambient backdrops remind the listener that the foursome could create their own world without compromising the tautness of the four corners of the band, be it watching from afar or pondering what is within. To further this intention, the interior sleeve included an excerpt from a piece entitled Jackie Pantomime: an autobiography:

'...and it was far from the mourning after.

'I was frequently feeling like I was in a film, that's when I was most relaxed. I'd become comfortable fidgeting in characters and roles, the fear lay in the prospect that the unrest would cease. It was only shortly after this that the name change came and I started with the face paint. I bullied the others into it really, Matt was the hardest to convince I remember, but we all became dependent on it eventually. I'd been in that house too long, we all had, what started off as something pretty to look at had become an obsession.

'It never occurred to us that too much time spent in a circus might lead to normality stealing its place in our perception. Burglars and clowns led by....'

Yet this book doesn't exist. It's entirely fictitious. One could surmise that Jackie Pantomime is a pseudonym for Alex Turner as the excerpt broadly fits into what we know about his style: writing from a different perspective suited him as it enabled him to be confessional without admitting as much. The name Jackie Pantomime would reappear soon, but in the meantime, the question was: would this new style appeal to the masses?

UK Album Chart – Top 10 – 29th April 2007:

1. ***Favourite Worst Nightmare* – Arctic Monkeys**
2. *Version* – Mark Ronson
3. *The Best Damn Thing* – Avril Lavigne
4. *Back To Black* – Amy Winehouse
5. *Everytime We Touch – The Album* – Cascada
6. *Like In Cartoon Motion* – Mika
7. *Because Of The Times* – Kings Of Leon
8. *B'Day* – Beyonce
9. *Loose* – Nelly Furtado
10. *Futuresex/Lovesounds* – Justin Timberlake

With some ease, the answer was categorically in the affirmative, even if *Favourite Worst Nightmare* didn't break records in the same vein as the first album. Although at 220,000 sales in the first week it was still the best-performing album of the year to date. In the same week, the entire album (and B-sides) made the top 200 of the Singles Charts, with five entries in the top 100: Brianstorm (7), Fluorescent Adolescent (60), 505 (74), Teddy Picker (94) and Temptation Greets You Like Your Naughty Friend (97). However, this was later put down to an error by iTunes, who had put all the tracks up for sale several hours before making the album available which, if nothing else, bore testament to the enthusiastic nature of fans who couldn't wait a few short hours. It also went straight in at number 7 on the Billboard charts.

The reviews were overwhelmingly positive, more so than before. The *NME* noticed its cinematic approach, declaring that '*Favourite Worst Nightmare* even subverts Hollywood's truism: the sequel's better,'(xxxi) while *The Guardian* felt the album showed them 'pushing gently but confidently at the boundaries of their sound'(xxxii). Even *Pitchfork* was warming to them, albeit through gritted teeth. In a mixed review, they ultimately decided that 'Arctic Monkeys may no longer belong to their old world of kids wearing 'knackered Converse', drinking underage, and getting accosted by bouncers, but they're still too boldly tuneful not to find yourself rooting for them'(xxxiii).

As was customary practice, the Japanese version of *Favourite Worst Nightmare* came with two bonus tracks, later released in the UK on download, and a limited edition 7" vinyl single to mark their headline appearance at Glastonbury Festival.

Single 5:

Matador/Da Frame 2R
Released: 18th June 2007; UK Chart Position: N/A; Label: Domino; Album: N/A

Track List: Matador; Da Frame 2R
Produced by: James Ford and Mike Crossey
All lyrics by Alex Turner; all music by Arctic Monkeys

The two tracks weren't up to the standard of songs on the album. Matador is largely instrumental with a four-bar beat and repetitive licks giving way to a slower tempo, a sequence of lyrics once again about a failed romance (possibly starring Jackie Pantomime) appearing in the last third of the song. More substantial (if shorter) is Da Frame 2R (pronounced Da Frame Tour, also known as The Frame to Relevance) with rolling drums and a staccato delivery from Turner about a handsome man who can get any girl he wants, so much so that '007 and Brucey Wayne are shitting there 'selves because there's another name coming to claim what is his to claim.'

CHAPTER SIX
'Frightened That Honesty Isn't Enough and it's Nothing on The Early Stuff.' (2007-2008)

In June 2007, Arctic Monkeys headlined Glastonbury Festival for the first time, playing on the Friday night to some 100,000 lucky punters. The set took place during one of the festival's muddiest ever years, but the rain didn't deter the band, who slipped in a cover of Shirley Bassey's Diamonds Are Forever as a tribute to the Welsh songstress (playing the much-heralded 'Legend' slot two days later).

In keeping with Glastonbury tradition, they brought two special guests onstage: Dizzee Rascal accompanied them for the maiden performance of their duet Temptation Greets You Like Your Naughty Friend; and Miles Kane, who provided additional guitar on 505, as on the record. Despite an impressive light show, the set suffered from sound problems but was largely well-received, although Alex Turner would later admit that it felt like a missed opportunity.

The setlist:

When the Sun Goes Down
Brianstorm
Still Take You Home
Dancing Shoes
From the Ritz to the Rubble
Teddy Picker
This House Is a Circus
Fake Tales Of San Francisco

Balaclava
Temptation Greets You Like Your Naughty Friend
Old Yellow Bricks
I Bet You Look Good on The Dancefloor
If You Were There, Beware
Fluorescent Adolescent
Mardy Bum
Do Me A Favour
Leave Before the Lights Come On
The View from The Afternoon
Diamonds Are Forever
505
A Certain Romance

The following week, the second official single was lifted from *Favourite Worst Nightmare.* The video for Fluorescent Adolescent was loosely inspired by the John Cooper Clarke poem *Out of Control Fairground* (reportedly Alex Turner's favourite), and featured two groups of men, one dressed as clowns, at an abandoned warehouse. The mid-section of the video features flashbacks of the two leaders of the groups as childhood friends, culminating in the clown leader killing his counterpart in the present day.

The clown leader, played by Stephen Graham, may have been Scummy Man, last seen aligning himself with a magician, although this was never confirmed. The video was directed by Richard Ayoade, best known at the time as one of the stars of Channel 4 comedy *The IT Crowd,* and the band adopted the clown motif when performing the song on *The Jonathan Ross Show*. Meanwhile, the single sleeve included a contribution from the song's protagonist with John Cooper Clarke drafting a new poem based on the character of the song.

Single 6:

Fluorescent Adolescent
Released: 4th July 2007; UK Chart Position: 5;
Label: Domino; Album: *Favourite Worst Nightmare*
B-Sides: The Bakery; Plastic Tramp; Too Much to Ask
Producers: James Ford and Mike Crossey
All tracks written by Alex Turner except Fluorescent Adolescent written by Alex Turner and Johanna Bennett

The Bakery is a ballad of sorts, the riff a similar version to the one found on Only Ones Who Know (albeit faster) and bringing Turner back to smalltown dreaming, watching an object of desire from afar in the titular bakery and other locations including, in keeping with the parent album's theme, an arcade. Plastic Tramp, meanwhile, is a driving rock song that directly addresses the cynicism certain people feel when encountering someone homeless: 'Is he really on the street? Desperation or deceit? And what he's wearing on his feet won't solve our mystery.'

Lastly, Too Much to Ask is another slow, but forgettable, romantic number. Written on the B-side of the vinyl record was the ominous warning: 'Sketchead is coming,' as the inclusion of three new songs ensured that Fluorescent Adolescent hit the Top 10 for its proper release.

UK Singles Chart – Top 10 – 15th July 2007:

1. Umbrella – Rihanna ft Jay-Z
2. Fergie – Big Girls Don't Cry

3. Foundations – Kate Nash
4. The Way I Are – Timbaland ft Doe/Keri Hilson
5. **Fluorescent Adolescent – Arctic Monkeys**
6. When You're Gone – Avril Lavigne
7. Do You Know – Enrique Iglesias
8. Worried About Ray – Hoosiers
9. Teenagers – My Chemical Romance
10. Soulmate – Natasha Bedingfield

Their second consecutive busy summer (a period in which Matt Helders announced his own fashion and apparel range *Supremebeing*) continued in July with the band's two big show dates at Old Trafford Cricket Ground. In an interview with *NME* during the build-up to the shows, Jamie Cook revealed that they expected their guestlist to be sizeable: 'I'm a bit worried now because every time we've played a gig in Sheffield lately, like the Leadmill, and people have been asking for tickets I've been saying, 'wait until Manchester, it will be alright,' and everyone's remembered! I'm never going to get everyone I said yes to on our list.' Nick O'Malley could match Cook's quota of 70 people, while Alex Turner was more ruthless; 'I've said, 'just send us a text the day beforehand.' They'll have a tantrum if they can't get in, there's nowt else they can do.'(xxxiv)

James Skelly, singer from support band The Coral, was confident the event would become legendary: 'I went to see The Verve at Haigh Hall in 1998 when I was a kid and I reckon this will rate up there for the kids here now.'(xxxv). Unfortunately, echoing their problems at Glastonbury, the sound cut out during the first show, but the band played on, unaware of the issue. The glitch was quickly remedied, and the remainder of the gig was declared a classic, with Alex Turner playfully goading the Lancashire crowd by encouraging those who had made the trip across the Pennines to chant their home county's name.

With 110,000 people in attendance across two nights, Arctic Monkeys successfully cemented their status as a huge live draw. To compound their achievements, *Favourite Worst Nightmare* was nominated for the Mercury Music prize, giving them the opportunity of being the first act to win the coveted prize in successive years, although they lost out to Klaxons' *Myths of The Near Future* (also produced by James Ford).

After their UK dates, Arctic Monkeys played international festivals in Australia, Japan, and Ibiza. Yet Alex Turner also managed to find time for a side project in France with his friend, Liverpudlian Miles Kane, latterly of The Little Flames and now lead songwriter with The Rascals. In an interview with *NME,* Kane provided some details on the project: 'We're there (France) for two weeks and we're going to try to get the majority of it done. James Ford is producing it and is going to play drums, he's a really boss drummer. Me and Al will do all the bass and guitar and vocal and try to get the bulk of it done in two weeks. We're going to record it quite live to tape, I think. Then whenever we've got weekends off at the same time we'd like to get some strings on it and probably do all that back home. That's the plan anyway.'(xxxvi) In the same interview, Kane also revealed the duo had the imaginative working title of Turner & Kane.

Elsewhere, following her support slot at the Old Trafford gigs, Arctic Monkeys returned the favour to Amy Winehouse by recording a cover of her track You Know I'm No Good for the second *Radio 1 Live*

Lounge album and, extending their tentacles further into the music community, found a new fan in Queens of The Stone Age frontman Josh Homme after the Monkeys supported them in Texas. While in the US, Arctic Monkeys debuted two new songs live: Sandtrap and Put Me in A Terror Pocket, a brace of songs that still await recorded releases.

Summer turned to autumn and awards season rolled around again. Despite losing out on the Mercury, Arctic Monkeys were still a strong presence across the season, picking up the Best Act in The World Today at the *Q* Awards, beating off stiff competition from U2, Muse, The Killers, and Foo Fighters. In addition, Alex Turner flew solo to pick up the Album Award at the Ivor Novello ceremony. Noting his embarrassment at accepting the award without his bandmates, when accepting the award he said, 'Whenever we've won things in the past, we've always just walked up here and mouthed off. We've always neglected to thank anybody so I would like to thank everybody now.'(xxxvii).

Some of their records were toppled at the same time, unfortunately, for later in the autumn the winner of the 2007 series of *The X Factor* (Leona Lewis) broke their record for fastest-selling debut album, her album *Spirit* shifting 12,000 more units in its first week. Meanwhile, back in Sheffield, former bassist Andy Nicholson had begun the process of dusting himself down and played DJ slots.

In September, electro-rock act Reverend and The Makers, fronted by old friend Jon McClure, released their debut album *The State of Things,* which included three contributions from Alex Turner. He takes lead vocals on The Machine (apart from the first verse, delivered by McClure) before the song becomes a duet while adding guitars on single, He

Said He Loved Me. Both tracks were credited to McClure/Turner, as was album closer Armchair Detective.

In late November, Domino released a limited-edition vinyl single (250 copies) by an outfit calling themselves The Death Ramps, accompanied by a press release that said, 'We're not allowed to tell you the true identity of The Death Ramps, but needless to say they're a band with A Certain Romance (wink wink).' The two tracks released were included in the package for the third and final single from *Favourite Worst Nightmare*: Teddy Picker. The name of this alter-ego was taken from the hills on which the band had ridden their BMXs as kids.

Single 7:

Teddy Picker
Released: 3rd December 2007; UK Chart Position: 20; Label: Domino; Album: *Favourite Worst Nightmare*
B-Sides: Bad Woman (featuring Richard Hawley); The Death Ramps; Nettles
Producers: James Ford and Mike Crossey
All tracks written by Alex Turner except Bad Woman written by Patrick Sickafus

The Death Ramps is a chunky, bass-driven instrumental while, in keeping with the childhood allusions, the raucous Nettles could be a story of a young man who has fallen in with the wrong crowd and allows himself to be bullied by them. Consequently, he either attempts to take his own life or is forced to do so; 'afterwards those spiky whispers said he brought his own rope……clinging to the doorframe he was dragged off to a reminder of where he had been.'

More cheerily, the remaining song, Bad Woman, was a moody and faithful cover, originally released in 1968 by Pat Farrell & The Believes, a garage rock outfit from Hamburg, Pennsylvania. The Monkeys' version featured the previously 'robbed' Richard Hawley on lead vocals. With a video directed by Roman Coppola, featuring the band recording a live version of the song at RAK studios in North London, Teddy Picker was the first Arctic Monkeys single that failed to break the top 10.

<u>UK Singles Chart – Top 10 – 9th December 2007:</u>

1. Bleeding Love – Leona Lewis
2. Heartbroken – T2 ft Jodie Aysha
3. Call The Shots – Girls Aloud
4. Apologize – Timbaland Ft One Republic
5. Rule The World – Take That
6. No One – Alicia Keys
7. Valerie – Mark Ronson ft Amy Winehouse
8. Mariah Carey – All I Want for Christmas Is You
9. Breathless – Shayne Ward
10. Crank That (Soulja Boy) – Soulja Boy Tellem

....

20. Teddy Picker – Arctic Monkeys

A triumphant year culminated in a short UK tour, with two nights each at the G-Mex in Manchester, Aberdeen's AECC, and Alexandra Palace in London, as well as a 'secret' gig at the Apollo, also in Manchester. The gigs were the band's longest to date, with Sandtrap, Put Me in A Terror Pocket, Da Frame 2R, Plastic Tramp, and Nettles all added alongside the majority of the first two albums. The Apollo gig was filmed and later released as a live album and DVD.

February 2008 saw Arctic Monkeys pick up more Brit Award nominations and, for the first time, the group and their entourage deigned to attend the ceremony, bringing their own irreverent twist. Adorned as country gents, the foursome took the opportunity to mock the Brit School (famously responsible for Adele, Kate Nash, Leona Lewis, and Amy Winehouse). Suitably refreshed, upon receiving the two awards (for Best Album and Best British Group) Turner, pointing at the front row, said, 'We all went to the Brit School, we remember you all!' Fearing a PR disaster, the TV coverage immediately went backstage as the group was shuffled offstage. The following week, at the *NME* awards, the group picked up Best British Band, Best Video (for Teddy Picker), and Best Track (Fluorescent Adolescent), three of a staggering six gongs for which they were nominated.

With the campaign for *Favourite Worst Nightmare* concluded and the shelf bulging from their awards, for the first time in some years Arctic Monkeys took a notable break, from the band at least, although two members continued to produce music. In keeping with his interest in beat-driven, electronic music, Matt Helders remixed tracks for a handful of artists, all of whom had either influenced or crossed paths with his band: Swedish garage-rockers The Hives (We Rule the World (T.H.E.H.I.V.E.S.)); Roots Manuva (Again & Again); Duran Duran (Skin Divers) and We Are Scientists (Chick Lit). In addition, he remixed Yo Majesty's Club Action, all of which presumably whet his appetite enough to spend the year working on a mix album.

Apparently not busy enough, and in addition to his dalliances in fashion, Helders also reignited his working relationship with Andy Nicholson. The former bassist had recovered from the blow of leaving one of Britain's biggest bands and had formed a hip-hop outfit along with Jon McClure, Joe Moskow, Babyshambles bassist Drew McConnell and London rapper Lowkey from the Poisonous Poets. Matt Helders appeared on two tracks from the group's debut EP *The Menace*: the title track and Barcode. He and Nicholson also found the time to open a pub in their native Sheffield, which they christened The Bowery.

But Helders wasn't the only busy Monkey, with the album that Alex Turner had been working on alongside Miles Kane and James Ford near completion. The duo, with Ford on drums and production, revealed that the name for their new project would be The Last Shadow Puppets, while their debut single and album shared the same name: *The Age of The Understatement*. With a sound hugely indebted to the 1960s, Arctic Monkeys fans may have been concerned that this might mean the end of the band and it was clear this was, at the very least, a different prospect. Turner and Kane had a stock uniform, often dressed in matching outfits such as smart, *A Hard Day's Night*-era Beatles suits, leather jackets, or roll-neck jumpers, complete with mod haircuts, and always wearing smart shoes such as Chelsea boots.

Alex Turner took steps to allay any fears fans may have had, explaining that he too felt some guilt: 'I thought it were going to be like finding a tape where you'd had an affair. Like your bird found an affair tape and was watching you having sex with another bird...but it weren't like an affair tape...not that I've ever made an affair tape.'

'The most dominant thing was just wanting to make a record with Miles Kane. I wasn't trying to fuck (the Monkeys) off at all. I love being in that band and they're my best mates.'(xxxix)

The Age of The Understatement featured a dual lead vocal from the singers over a cantering, string-driven mini-epic in the style of Ennio Morricone which may feature guitar from Kane but is by no means the focus. The video highlighted the distance between this project and Turner's main band: shot in Moscow by Romain Gavras, it featured Turner and Kane walking through the Russian capital, sometimes flanked by soldiers and tanks in mid-winter snow, and quite different from the studio setting of Alex Turner's most recent video, three months earlier. Backed with the rocky Two Hearts in Two Weeks and two covers (Wondrous Place, first released by Jimmy Jones in May 1960 but made famous by Billy Fury in September of the same year, and David Bowie's In the Heat of The Morning from 1968), the single made the top 10 in April 2008.

The Last Shadow Puppets: Debut Single:

The Age of The Understatement
Released: 14th April 2008; UK Chart Position: 9;
Label: Domino; Album: *The Age of The Understatement*
B-Sides: Two Hearts in Two Weeks; Wondrous Place; In the Heat of The Morning
Producer: James Ford
All tracks written by Alex Turner and Miles Kane, except Wondrous place written by Lewis/Giant, and In the Heat of The Morning written by David Bowie

Patronage for In the Heat of The Morning came from no less a source than the great man himself, David Bowie, who declared on his website: 'That's a delight! How lovely. A daymaker.'(xl) The album was released the following week and went in at number 1 in the Album Chart, completing a hat-trick for Alex Turner.

The Last Shadow Puppets: Debut Album:

The Age of The Understatement
Released: 21 April 2008; UK Chart Position: 1; Label: Domino
Track Listing: The Age of the Understatement; Standing Next to Me; Calm Like You; Separate and Every Deadly; The Chamber; Only the Truth; My Mistakes Were Made for You; Black Plant; I Don't Like You Anymore; In My Room; Meeting Place; Time Has Come Again
Producer: James Ford
All lyrics by Alex Turner and Miles Kane

If nothing else, *The Age of The Understatement* gave Alex Turner, as a pure songwriter, the opportunity to focus less on band-orientated material and instead on different musical textures. Alternatively, it could simply be because he was so prolific (as songwriters tend to be early in their careers), and he was churning songs out at such a rate that one band wasn't enough for him.

The whole album is driven by strings, and the influences that he and Kane cited (Scott Walker, Serge Gainsbourg, Ennio Morricone, The Electric Prunes) can all be clearly heard and were very obviously on rotation during the album's recording sessions in France (Black Box Studios) and London (RAK Studios). Perhaps flexing their muscles, the London Metropolitan Orchestra was brought in to provide the grandiosity the songs required.

The Age of The Understatement is an immersive album, it's symphonic pop (with strings arranged by Owen Pallet, able to count Arcade Fire among his previous clients) so out of step with everything else prevalent in guitar music in 2008. Sequenced well, some songs gallop (Separate and Ever Deadly, Calm Like You, the title track), while others allow the listener to pause for contemplation (The Chamber, The Meeting Place) or consume everything in sight with the sheer drama (I Don't Like You Anymore, Only the Truth). John Barry is clearly a key influence too, as many tracks share similar traits to those in the James Bond canon. Turner and Kane's harmonies are superb throughout, although it is sometimes hard to differentiate between the two young men, so similar are their voices.

Of the two singers, Alex Turner is more dominant across the album, taking lead vocals on three numbers (Calm Like You, My Mistakes Were Made for You, Time Has Come Again) while Kane supports him on two others (The Chamber, Black Plant). Only on the superb Standing Next to Me does the Liverpudlian take lead vocals, with every other song splitting the vocals evenly, as are the entirety of the writing credits.

If we must make the comparison, Time Has Come Again is very much in line with the melancholic romance of Only Ones Who Know, while I Don't Like You Anymore could sit on *Favourite Worst Nightmare* with its drawn-out, piano-led tones. Regardless, it's remarkable to think that its release came just over two years after *Whatever People Say I Am, That's*

What I'm Not. To add to the retro vibe, the cover image was a shot of a model taken by Sam Haskins in 1962, and the album was nominated for the Mercury Award, Alex Turner's third in a row.

The Last Shadow Puppets played a handful of shows in the spring and summer of 2008 in promotion, including a secret acoustic set at Glastonbury on the Park Stage, with guests including Matt Helders (on drums for the title track) and Jack White, adding a solo on Wondrous Place. This was followed by two gigs, in Portsmouth and Oxford, where the group was backed by a 16-piece orchestra, and an appearance at the *NME* tent Reading & Leeds festival at the end of the summer.

Two further singles were lifted from *The Age of The Understatement:* Standing Next to Me hit number 30 in July while My Mistakes Were Made for You failed to crack the Top 40, only making number 81 in November. Both were accompanied by videos directed by Richard Ayoade while My Mistakes Were Made for You included a live version of Paris Summer featuring a guest appearance by Alison Mosshart from The Kills. The Last Shadow Puppets peppered their live shows with covers: Little Red Book (a live cover) was originally a cover of the Burt Bacharach/Hal David 1965 single; Paris Summer was originally by Lee Hazlewood and Nancy Sinatra and the group also covered tracks by The Beatles (I Want You [She's So Heavy]) and Leonard Cohen (Memories) in their live shows.

The Last Shadow Puppets: Second Single:

Standing Next to Me
Released: 7th July 2008; UK Chart Position: 30; Label: Domino; Album: *The Age Of The*

Understatement
B-Sides: Hang the Cyst; Gas Dance; Sequels
Producer: James Ford

The Last Shadow Puppets: Third Single:

My Mistakes Were Made for You
Released: 20th October 2008; UK Chart Position: 81; Label: Domino; Album: *The Age of The Understatement*
B-Sides: Paris Summer (live from the Olympia Theatre, Paris); Separate and Ever Deadly (live from New Theatre, Oxford); My Little Red Book (live from New Theatre, Oxford)
Producer: James Ford
All songs written by Alex Turner and Miles Kane except Paris Summer (Hazlewood) and My Little Red Book (David/Bacharach)

A creatively and commercially satisfying venture for both (and a useful leg-up for Kane), The Last Shadow Puppets wrapped up their commitments with tours of the US and UK which included a show at Liverpool's Philharmonic Hall as part of the BBC Electric Proms. Meanwhile, as a welcome bonus and boost to Turner's classic songwriter status, legendary crooner Tony Christie covered Only Ones We Know for his collection of covers, *Made in Sheffield.*

Meanwhile Matt Helders' mix album was released in October 2008. Part of the *Late Night Tales* series, whose previous contributors included The Flaming Lips, Groove Armada and Fatboy Slim, it included some of Helders' favourite tracks and others that reflected the mood of the line. The album, credited to both Matt Helders and Arctic Monkeys, profiled the drummer's eclectic tastes, and included two new compositions: a reworked version of 1995 hit single Dreamer by Livin' Joy, which Helders gave an acid-electro fleck to, and a short story written and read by Alex Turner.

Matt Helders – Mix Tape Album:

Late Night Tales: Matt Helders
Released: 27th October 2008; UK Chart Position: N/A; Label: Azuli
Track Listing: Connexion (Goblin); Vaudeville (Viktor Vaughn); Yama Yama (Yamasuki); Play The Drum (Zeph & Azeem); Charity Shop Soundclash (DJ Format ft Aspects); Free Salute (Little Barrie); Thickfreakness (The Black Keys); Dreamer (Matt Helders ft Nesreen Shah); Dirt (The Stooges); Sheba (Johnny & The Hurricanes); The Dark Side Of The Sun (Modeselektor ft Puppetmastaz); Ms. Fat Booty (Mos Def); I Got 5 On It (Original Clean Short Mix) (Luniz); Grey Harpoon (The Coral); Reasons (Minnie Riperton); Dreamy Days (Roots Manuva); Break The Lock (Ty); I Believe (Simian Mobile Disco); Olio (The Rapture); Interlude; A Choice Of Three (Alex Turner)

In the same period, Matt Helders gave an update on the status of their third album for his parent band, disclosing that they had been recording with Josh Homme at his Joshua Tree studio in California: 'We did a few days in the desert and it was amazing. The studio is just like a house that's converted into a studio, but the area surrounding it; you've never really seen anything like it. Before we went, he (Homme) was saying that special things happen there. We were like, 'What can he mean?' But it really had quite an effect on us.'(xli). Helders had also teamed up with James O'Hara, the third owner of The Bowery, to start formulating plans for a festival in their native Sheffield, which later became Tramlines.

As 2008 ended, Arctic Monkeys squeezed in a release for the Christmas market. The package for *Arctic Monkeys at The Apollo* included a DVD of the band's performance in Manchester one year earlier as well as an LP release from a gig in Texas back in 2006. The concert film was shot on super 16 mm, the noise of the crowd reduced to as minimal a volume as possible to ensure the band's performance could be properly heard.

A co-production between Warp Films, Domino Records, and Bang Bang Films, directed by Richard Ayoade and photographed by cinemaphotographer Danny Cohen, the title referenced the legendary series of albums 'recorded live at Harlem's world-famous Apollo Theater'. Embracing the technology, the DVD included an option to watch Matt Helders' performance in 'Multi-Angle Camera View,' a treat for the drummer's following. As part of the promotion, the four members of the band and Ayoade engaged in a press conference before its screening at the Rex Theatre near Leicester Square, London.

Live Album 1/DVD:

Arctic Monkeys at the Apollo
Released: 3rd November 2008; UK Chart Position: N/A; Label: Domino
Track Listing (DVD): Brianstorm; This House Is a

Circus; Teddy Picker; I Bet You Look Good on the Dancefloor; Dancing Shoes; From the Ritz to the Rubble; Fake Tales of San Francisco; When the Sun Goes Down; Nettles; D Is for Dangerous; Leave Before the Lights Come On; Fluorescent Adolescent; Still Take You Home; Da Frame 2R; Plastic Tramp (with Miles Kane); 505 (with Miles Kane); Do Me a Favour; A Certain Romance; The View from the Afternoon; If You Were There, Beware. Bonus Tracks: Balaclava; Bad Woman (feat. Richard Hawley)

LP: Live in Texas – 7th June 2006
Track Listing: Riot Van; The View from the Afternoon; Still Take You Home; You Probably Couldn't See for The Lights but You Were Staring Straight At Me; Cigarette Smoker Fiona; Perhaps Vampires Is A Bit Strong But...; Dancing Shoes; I Bet You Look Good On The Dancefloor; When The Sun Goes Down; A Certain Romance

CHAPTER SEVEN
'Fools On Parade Cavort and Carry on For Waiting Eyes' (2009-2010)

While his former bandmates were recording their third album, Andy Nicholson and Mongrel released their debut (and to date only) album: *Better Than Heavy/Better Than Dub*. The collective took the unusual step of giving their electro-hip-hop album away for free to readers of *The Independent* newspaper on Saturday 7th March 2009 before a traditional CD release followed 16 days later. Unfortunately, Nicholson's luck in the music industry wasn't to improve, as the album had a muted, if not non-existent, response despite the presence of his drumming friend. In truth, the album was too politically charged to break the mainstream during a relatively politically stable time, the effects of the 2008 financial crisis still too fresh to truly see.

Meanwhile, Nicholson's former bandmates spent the autumn of 2008 at Josh Homme's Rancho de la Luna Studios, laying down an initial 12 songs for consideration for their third album. In an interview with John Kennedy of XFM, Helders and Turner gave some insight into the collaboration: 'We'd met Josh a couple of times from playing with (his band). He listened to the demos and said, 'let's do this, come to the desert.' Quick as a flash, Turner interrupted with his trademark dry wit, 'We thought we were going for a knickerbocker glory.'

Their spell in California was followed by further sessions in Brooklyn in the spring of 2009, with James Ford back on production duties. In between, Arctic Monkeys headed to Australia and

New Zealand for a short tour, taking the opportunity to road-test some of their new songs including Pretty Visitors, Go-Kart (which would become Potion Approaching), Dangerous Animals and Crying Lightning, as well as a cover of Nick Cave and the Bad Seeds' 1994 single Red Right Hand.

Having not played a gig for over a year, it was the first sighting of the band's latest look, all with longer hair (Helders aside), the tidy regulation Mod haircuts having grown out to become shoulder-length with fringes covering their eyes, while their moodier, sludgy psychedelic-rock sound, garnished with slide guitar and piano, was met with a mixed response. On their return to the UK, Arctic Monkeys picked up their by-now mandatory *NME* Award: *At The Apollo* picked up Best DVD while Turner pocketed a second award, Best Video for The Last Shadow Puppets' My Mistakes Were Made for You.

The group, represented by Matt Helders, released a video message just before Christmas 2008, the drummer giving an update on the band's recent activity, which led to Arctic Monkeys releasing a series of video diaries from January on their YouTube channel. Highlighting their irreverent humour and shot by James Ford on his phone, the first set of videos, dubbed *The View From....* (The Barbershop, The Laundry Room, The Dressing Room, The Marriott Spa, The Orange Stage) featured Helders diarising their antics while in Australia (for the Big Day Out Festival) with O'Malley as his comic foil. Turner featured minimally, only ever making Margherita cocktails, while Cook featured even less, only dancing silently in sunglasses.

Later videos included studio updates and clips of the band in rehearsals in London, briefly playing Poker Face by Lady Gaga, while another showed the burgeoning friendship between Helders and rapper P Diddy, appearing in a video entitled *The View from Sean's House Party.* The clips tantalised fans with snippets of new material while also announcing that they would be joined onstage by John Ashton on keys. Meanwhile, on the last day of the third album sessions, the photograph which would become the album's cover was taken.

After being announced as headliners for the Reading & Leeds festival in March, Arctic Monkeys revealed the track listing (albeit not the title) for the new album in July 2009. In accompanying interviews, Alex Turner revealed that a notebook containing the album's lyrics had been stolen but felt that the incident benefitted the songs: 'I went the morning after and bought a couple of Moleskines and sat around for a couple of hours trying to remember it all. But I found the whole process made me write more things, complete things that I wouldn't have otherwise.'(xlii)

Elsewhere, in an interview with *GQ* magazine, album producer Josh Homme lavished praise on the band, specifically their lyricist and drummer. 'I was sucked in at first by the lyrics. Alex sounded like a rare poet playing music – he has a special gift for the gab,' said the Queens of The Stone Age frontman, also pronouncing Helders as 'one of the best drummers in rock 'n' roll.' Eulogising the forthcoming album, Homme declared, 'This is the record where they get weird, grow up, and trip out.'

Speaking to Radio 1's *Newsbeat*, the album's other producer warned of changes afoot. 'It'll definitely surprise people, especially people who are familiar with things like ...Dancefloor and stuff like that, they might be quite taken aback,' said James Ford. 'They're progressing and moving forward trying to change, push themselves and push their audience which I think is rare in a lot of bands today. They've just got more relaxed with themselves – they're comfortable doing what they're doing...'(xliii)

The first half of 2009 wasn't entirely devoid of Arctic Monkeys-related material, with Matt Helders appearing on two tracks from rapper Toddla T's album, (Boom D.J. and Better) released in May. Then, on 6th July 2009, after much anticipation, Radio 1's Zane Lowe gave the Arctic Monkeys' new single its first play. After reported deliberation, the song chosen to herald the new era was Crying Lightning.

Single 8:

Crying Lightning
Released: 6th July 2009 (digital download), 17 August 2009 (vinyl release); UK Chart Position: 12; Label: Domino; Album: *Humbug*
B-Sides: Red Right Hand; I Haven't Got My Strange
Producer: Josh Homme
All tracks written by Alex Turner except Red Right Hand (Mick Harvey/Nick Cave/Thomas Wydler)

The single was made available on digital download a few hours after its radio debut and was therefore immediately eligible for the UK Singles Chart the following Sunday before a vinyl-only physical release followed on 17th August 2009. The vinyl was released on two formats, a 10" and a 7", the latter of which was only available through branches of Oxfam with the band encouraging the donation of clothing or music memorabilia when purchasing the single.

UK Singles Chart – Top 10 - 12th July 2009:

1. Evacuate The Dancefloor – Cascada
2. Bulletproof – La Roux
3. Man In the Mirror – Michael Jackson
4. Paparazzi – Lady Gaga
5. When Love Takes Over – David Guetta ft Kelly Rowland
6. Diamond Rings – Chipmunk ft Emeli Sande
7. Boom Pow – Black Eyed Peas
8. Knock You Down – Keri Hilson/Kanye West/Ne-Yo
9. Release Me – Agnes
10. I Gotta Feeling – Black Eyed Peas

....

12. Crying Lightning – Arctic Monkeys

Although the single fell short of the top 10, its position just outside at number 12 was respectable given it was only available in one format. As an entry point for this much-vaunted new era, Crying Lightning works well, the song exploding into life as the band starts as one, with Nick O'Malley's stiff, almost electro-bass lusty in its desire (memorably described by Josh Homme as 'a fat kid with chocolate on his face,'). Helders' drum fills never overstep the mark, just the right side of flamboyant, while Cook subtly underfills Turner's rhythm guitar, whose subdued vocals for the first chorus and verse mark the song's tone, and when he changes key from the second verse onwards, the mood conveyed changes with him.

Despite the new desert-American sound, Alex Turner's lyrics are still firmly entrenched in the UK. References to sweets abound: 'pick and mix,' 'strawberry lace' and 'gobstopper,' as well as 'the ice cream man,' represent an innocent, playful nature to the antagonist (as well as foreshadowing the incoming album) of the song but hinting there is more than meets the eye and Turner knows it. 'Your pastimes consisted of the strange and twisted and deranged and I hate that little game you had called 'Crying Lightning."' The protagonist has fallen for a girl who he knows is bad news, but intrigue and desire overcome reason, even if he knows it will end in heartbreak.

I Haven't Got My Strange feels like a hangover from *Favourite Worst Nightmare.* Though heavier in sound, it features an imploring vocal performance from Turner and veers in several different directions, lightweight in comparison to what would come. Better, and more telling, is their bruising, stinging cover of Red Right Hand. Its composer, Nick Cave, drew inspiration from the poem *Paradise Lost* by John Milton, in which the 'red right hand' represents divine vengeance, a heady theme which Turner could draw parallels with.

Richard Ayoade was assigned directorial duties for the video, which portrayed the band in a quasi-surreal world on a boat at sea. The boat sails as the band plays, before a larger-than-life version of Turner emerges from the sea for the guitar solo, later joined by his bandmates. The nautical theme would be one of many on *Humbug.*

The new era of Arctic Monkeys had begun. Gone were the indie boys next door in their casual clothing, replaced by long-haired, leather-clad rock stars. Many would struggle to adapt to the change but there was no going back, as Crying Lightning's parent album would emphatically prove.

Album 3:

Humbug
Released: 19th August 2009; UK Chart Position: 1; Label: Domino
Track Listing: My Propeller; Crying Lightning; Dangerous Animals; Secret Door; Potion Approaching; Fire and the Thud; Cornerstone; Dance Little Liar; Pretty Visitors; The Jeweller's Hands
Producers: Joshua Homme (Tracks 2/3/5/6/8/9/10), James Ford (1/4/7)

For a few brief seconds, as My Propeller rattles the earlobes, the listener is in familiar territory, but the band is toying with expectations. The familiarity is brief as a sense of brooding doom takes over in the form of the opening riff. Less immediate but no less exciting, the lumbering opening sets the mood for a darker, more intense album, the wonky guitar adding to the sense of discombobulation. Instilled with new heft and gravitas, Turner sings in a hushed manner, going for the soul where he once went for the jugular. 'If you can summon the strength, tow me,' he asks.

The obvious metaphor for the propeller is Turner's penis, but that seems too coarse and obvious for a writer so talented (he would also later categorically deny such an implication). Rather, the propeller is his mood or mojo, which needs the inspiration to fly again and is coercing someone to help him with it, perhaps not entirely truthfully. My Propeller is understated, but still contains the tempo changes which were the band's trademark but delivers them less frantically while still forcibly.

After the enthralling Crying Lightning, the brutal march of Dangerous Animals tramples over the hill, opening with what sounds like an uncredited vocal by Homme for the opening seconds. A romping blitzkrieg with stacked vocals builds to a crescendo of spelling out the title, which perfectly highlights Matt Helders' importance as the backbone of Arctic Monkeys.

The lead actor in this piece is completely beguiled and has 'been fighting with my sheets and nearly crying in my sleep,' while being 'pinned down by the dark', powerless to confront the titular animals. Possibly inspired by Leopold von Sacher-Masoch's novella *Venus in Furs* (which also inspired The Velvet Underground's song of the same name), he sado-masochistically implores her to put her out of his misery: 'It's been long enough now, so let's make a mess, lioness.'

Secret Door threatens to return proceedings to a more recognisable footing, and indeed does evolve to culminate in a swooning lift-off, but not before some more wiry guitar and relentless drums intersperse the familiarity. The mood of the song is almost lethargic until it becomes a full-on, lighters-in-the-air ballad. Lyrically, it refers to celebrity culture, its demands (at this point Turner was in a relationship with presenter Alexa Chung and therefore tabloid fodder), and how uncomfortable it makes him feel.

The 'fools on parade' are possibly the celebrities and, one step ahead as ever, they even 'conduct a singalong', like this song was designed to. Self-deprecating but also knowing that his partner has 'never been the kind to be hollowed out by the stares,' they both seek refuge behind their secret door.

Moving away from matters of the heart, Potion Approaching takes the riff from Very Ape by Nirvana, sprinkles it with acid, and garnishes it with metallic percussion and a sneering vocal. The use of analogies is stretched to breaking point and veers towards nonsensical ('yours is the only ocean I wanna swing from,'), but may make sense when under the influence of a potion ('I preferred her as a cartoon,'). The influence of Homme is in full flow here, the slowed-down mid-section of 'oohs' very akin to Queens of The Stone Age as well as a nod to The Rolling Stones' Sympathy for The Devil.

Featuring a guest appearance from Alison Mosshart (best known as the singer from The Kills) on backing vocals, the languid Fire and the Thud is eerily tentative before squawking into life in the third minute. Unquestionably about love, perhaps at first sight, an acoustic version of the track kicked around before it was given the full band treatment. Initially underwhelming, after several listens, it burrows under the skin.

After an intense rock quagmire, the clouds open with the arrival of Cornerstone, in the form of *Revolver*-era Beatles backward guitars which herald perhaps Alex Turner's best song (certainly the best-realised). Musically it's quite conventional, but the lyrics are, not to overstate matters, astonishing, with a level of detail unlike anything seen before. The narrator goes from pub to pub, all of which have pirate-themed names, invoking the concept that the girl he is looking for is a lost treasure.

The lyrics take the form of a short story, as his search becomes increasingly desperate, until he eventually finds the subject matter's sister, which provides a happy conclusion of sorts: 'I thought she might understand that she was close, well you couldn't get much closer, she said, 'I'm really not supposed to but yes, you can call me anything you want." In addition, that resolution ties into the album's theme of deception and falsehoods, while the last chorus is subtly extended by a few bars to incorporate 'well you couldn't get much closer.' It's an outlier on the album as the rest of the band serves the song rather than overloading it, as if they are as entranced by Turner's lyrics as the listener. Stunning.

The album's main theme is presented most emphatically on the multi-layered Dance Little Liar: 'And the clean coming will hurt and you can never get it spotless, when there's dirt beneath the dirt the liar takes a lot less time,'. Meanwhile, the anticipation ratchets up via the rapid-fire tom-tom/bass drumming and a solo that sounds like a fire alarm, one of the many layers of instrumentation. A release of energy in the final third climaxes the song before a snarling coda and then, unusually, a fade-out.

The oldest song in spirit and delivery on *Humbug* is Pretty Visitors, with a staccato of rapid-fire lyrics sneeringly spat out by Turner, but the music beneath the lyrics is hugely different from what once was; a crunching, mighty rock symphony with a selectively used organ that adds to another carnival atmosphere, as garnered through the lyrics. One of the harder songs to interpret seems to be an analogy of the pretty visitors attending a circus (perhaps a call back to the previous album) which may refer to the fans at the band's gigs. The 'chicken or the dickhead' perhaps poses a question about the make-up of their audience and the group's wider appeal. Pretty Visitors is a culmination of the three Arctic Monkeys albums to date, with breathless delivery (*Whatever People Say I Am, That's What I'm Not),* organs, and talk of carnivals (*Favourite Worst*

Nightmare) but with a much heavier sound. Likely only Alex Turner knows the true meaning of the song.

The carnival theme extends into the opening line of closer The Jeweller's Hands ('fiendish wonder in the carnival's wake,'). Lyrically obtuse but later clarified by Turner himself, the song is about an illicit affair that gets out of hand ('move toward the danger that you seek,' 'You thought you'd never get obsessed,'), with the jeweller's methodical approach beguiling. A slice of epic melancholia, it unsettles then floats away like an ellipsis, or outwards towards the murky sea, marking the continuation of an already eventful journey.

Humbug marked a turning point in Arctic Monkeys' careers and is now regarded as necessary in their evolution. A valid point but one which ignores the album itself, loaded as it is with themes and analogies rendering it very nearly indecipherable. The nautical (Cornerstone, the video for Crying Lightning) and carnival themes support an overall concept of deception and falsehoods (as per the title) with Turner's use of metaphors taken to an unprecedented level.

Broadly speaking, it comes back to tales of the heart and body, but the limited subject matter is expanded upon through witticisms and poetry rather than direct narration, while musically sturdier and more boisterous than before. One of those albums that time has been kind to, *Humbug* reveals more layers with every listen. With hindsight, it's little surprise that the album received such a mixed response. They were bravely challenging their audience in every way.

Despite its use of metaphors and characters, Alex Turner confirmed in a promotional interview with the *NME* that his writing had become more honest. When asked if the songs were about him, he replied, 'Yeah. But not unanimously. There's a bit of it all. Sometimes I did start out writing something and think, 'I want to take the traditional approach to this'...I suppose you can't but help become familiar with writing about this entity of thing that is this extension of this situation that has happened, or that you would like to happen. It's just a whole load of words disguising one phrase in the centre that is something that you do want to say.'

If this seems disarmingly honest from the previously reluctant songwriter, both the album's title and Turner's previously flexible approach to honesty in interviews are worth remembering. In the same interview, Jamie Cook confirmed the effect the new recording location had: 'the desert definitely did make a better environment, and definitely introduced possibilities that wouldn't have been there without it.'(xliv)

Fan opinions were (and continue to be) split on the album but, perhaps not wanting to appear unable to grasp the album's complexities, the music press was positive. *The Guardian* observed that the album was 'the work of a band with enough nous to realise they will never again be what they once were: a phenomenal success that temporarily unites everyone from people who buy LPs in Tesco to rock hacks.' The same review also predicted that 'Arctic Monkeys' best might be yet to come.'(xlv)

Pitchfork, meanwhile, was slowly coming around but still hard to please, deciding that '*Humbug* isn't better than either of its predecessors, but it expands the group's range and makes me curious where it might go next.'(xlvi) Lastly, the *NME* correctly pondered the reaction the album would receive while also slyly referencing the band's earlier prediction:

'Arctic Monkeys have reached the point where the people who love them a lot will clutch them ever closer to their hears, and the people who kinda liked 'em will be wondering who the fuck they are in five years time.'(xlvii)

Four days after the album's release, the band played their first UK dates in two years. First up, a warm-up date at Brixton Academy with support coming from Them Crooked Vultures, a new project featuring Homme on guitar, Foo Fighters' Dave Grohl on drums, and John Paul Jones, best known as the bassist from Led Zeppelin. Days afterwards was the small matter of their first headline slots at Reading & Leeds festival, with a headline slot in Yorkshire on Friday night the first set, which took place as their former hero Noel Gallagher was leaving Oasis.

The Saturday slot, broadcast live on BBC TV, was the first time that much of their home country had seen this new, heavier, hard-hitting version of the band. Not ordinarily gregarious, Turner was quiet throughout the set, rarely thanking the 'ladies and gentlemen' in attendance as he had done on previous occasions. It did little to defuse accusations of inaccessibility, the band looking almost disinterested when playing older songs, which included a longer, beefier version of Still Take You Home. However, Turner would later claim that they had enjoyed the show more than any before, these fools on parade doing their best to conduct a singalong or two.

The setlist was:

My Propellor
Red Right Hand
Crying Lightning
Brianstorm

Still Take You Home
I Bet You Look Good on The Dancefloor
Potion Approaching
Pretty Visitors
This House Is a Circus
If You Were There, Beware
When The Sun Goes Down
Dangerous Animals
The View from The Afternoon
Cornerstone
Only Ones Who Know
Do Me A Favour
Fluorescent Adolescent (with Dion's Only You Know snippet)
Secret Door
505

Capping a successful weekend, *Humbug* entered the UK Album Chart at Number One, shortly before they announced a UK arena tour (their first).

UK Album Chart – Top 10 – 30th August 2009:

1. ***Humbug* – Arctic Monkeys**
2. *One Love* – David Guetta
3. *Ready For the Weekend* – Calvin Harris
4. *The End* – Black Eyed Peas
5. *Catch 22* – Tinchy Stryder
6. *Sunny Side Up* – Paolo Nutini
7. *I Am Sasha Fierce* – Beyonce
8. *The Essential* – Michael Jackson
9. *Songs For You, Truths for Me* – James Morrison
10. *Lungs* – Florence & The Machine

Back in 2007, Arctic Monkeys contributed to a new project by their friends Shane Meadows and Paddy Considine. A mock documentary with improvised performances, *Le Donk & Scor-zay-zee* was shot over five days leading up to the band's gigs at Old Trafford Cricket Ground. Also starring Dean Palinczuk, Olivia Colman, and Meadows himself, it featured cameo appearances from Matt Helders and Nick O'Malley, along with a brief appearance by the whole group.

The film was released in October 2009 with a premiere at the 2009 Edinburgh Festival. An entertaining watch, it's also notable by the changes in the appearance of the group members in two years. In the same month, as they were touring the US, Arctic Monkeys announced their second single from *Humbug.* The video for Cornerstone (directed by Richard Ayoade) featured only Alex Turner singing the lyrics into a microphone with cassette recorder against a white backdrop (wearing a red jumper that would later become a plot point of *Submarine*) and premiered a few days after the announcement.

Single 9:

Cornerstone
Released: 16th November 2009; UK Chart Position: 94; Label: Domino; Album: *Humbug*
B-Sides: Catapult; Sketchead; Fright Lined Dining Room
Producer: James Ford

The single, which once again had a vinyl release in Oxfam stores, was backed by three new songs. The sprightly Catapult is about a man who's 'turned your legs to building blocks and with his index finger flicks you on your socks,' and, although lighter than most of *Humbug,* was perhaps too similar in subject matter to sit on the album. Similarly, Sketchead, who's coming had been foreshadowed since Fluorescent Adolescent, is about a man who can deceive easily (being 'sketched' is to be fooled) whereas the narrator, 'approached you like you were the same.' The song has a less dense feel, more like tracks from the previous era, and charted higher (80) than Cornerstone (94).

Lastly, the menacing Fright Lined Dining Room is comparatively direct, recalling a time when the lead observed the punters in a strip club, possibly inspired during the time of the album's recording ('And meanwhile in the desert's only costume shop the cowls hang and wait to rot away the identities of the willing').

UK Singles Chart – Top 10 – 22nd November 2009

1. You Are Not Alone – X Factor Finalists 2009
2. Meet Me Halfway – Black Eyed Peas
3. Whatcha Say – Jason Derulo
4. Happy – Leona Lewis
5. Fight For This Love – Cheryl Cole
6. Everybody In Love – JLS
7. Tik Tok – Kesha
8. Bad Romance – Lady Gaga
9. I Need You – N-Dubz
10. 3 – Britney Spears

……………………………………………

94. Cornerstone – Arctic Monkeys

Amid their UK arena shows and a lengthy US tour, Alex Turner supported Richard Hawley at an acoustic show at the Union Chapel in London for one night, part of the Mencap Little Noise charity shows. As well as debuting future B-side Joining the Dots, Turner premiered another new song entitled Glass in The Park, while being joined by Jamie Cook on guitar for Secret Door and Cornerstone. Turner also took the opportunity to play a full version of Dion's Only You Know and another cover, I Don't Want to Set the World on Fire by The Ink Spots.

The new decade started with a European tour and an unprecedented seven nominations at the 2010 *NME* Awards: Best British Band, Best Live Band, Best Album, Best Track (Crying Lightning), Best Video (Cornerstone), the Giving It Back award (for their Oxfam initiative), with Alex Turner also picking up a nod for Hero of The Year. The singer wasn't in attendance but Nick O'Malley and Matt Helders, complete with a new bouffant, were there to pick up the award for Best Live Act, the group's only win. A few weeks later came the third and final single from *Humbug.*

Initially proposed as Pretty Visitors, the group instead opted for the first track from the album with a psychedelic, black-and-white video. The single was backed with a further three new songs: the wonky Joining the Dots, the cantering The Afternoon's Hart, and Don't Forget Whose Legs You're On, a ragged, jangly track held together by an insistent simple piano. All seemed to deal with matters of the heart once more.

Single 10:

My Propeller
Released: 22nd March 2010; UK Chart Position: 90;
Label: Domino; Album: *Humbug*
B-Sides: Joining the Dots; The Afternoon's Hat;
Don't Forget Whose Legs You're On
Producer: James Ford

UK Singles Chart – Top 10 – 28th March 2010:

1. Telephone – Lady Gaga ft Beyonce
2. Pass Out – Tinie Tempah
3. Baby – Justin Bieber ft Ludacris
4. Rude Boy – Rihanna
5. Parachute – Cheryl Cole
6. Hot – Inna
7. Starry Eyed – Ellie Goulding
8. In My Head – Jason Derulo
9. Bedrock – Young Money ft Lloyd
10. Gave It All Away – Boyzone

……………………………………………………

90. Arctic Monkeys – My Propeller

To wrap up the campaign for their third album, Arctic Monkeys played a set for the Teenage Cancer Trust at the Royal Albert Hall in London and then an unannounced show at Shepherd's Bush Empire the following night, before venturing Stateside once more in the spring of 2010.

CHAPTER EIGHT
'I Took the Batteries Out My Mysticism And Put 'Em In My Thinking Cap' (2010-2011)

After the *Humbug* tour concluded in Mexico, the members of Arctic Monkeys pursued other projects for the remainder of 2010. Matt Helders took the opportunity to make more music with Andy Nicholson, the pair collaborating on three songs (Voice, Be Together and End Is the Beginning) as part of the fundraising group The Bottletop Band, while also temporarily filling in on drums for his new friend P Diddy's backing band (Dirty-Diddy Money) for a performance of the rapper's single Hello Good Morning on *The Jonathan Ross Show.*

Elsewhere, friend of the band Richard Ayoade started work on a film, a coming-of-age melancholy drama set in Welsh suburbia entitled *Submarine,* his directorial debut. Ayoade approached Alex Turner to enquire if he would be interested in recording new versions of tracks by Jacques Brel and Scott Walker, but Turner instead offered to produce one new composition, which eventually became five.

With James Ford on production and mixing, and additional instrumentation from The Coral's former guitarist Bill Ryder-Jones and Owen Pallett (string arrangement), the *Submarine* EP was released on 14 March 2011, six months after the film's premiere at Toronto International Film Festival.

Based on the debut novel of the same name by Joe Dunthorne, the film follows a neurotic 15-year-old struggling to lose his virginity while also trying to derail his parent's imminent divorce.

Starring Craig Roberts, Yasmin Page, Sally Hawkins, Noah Taylor, and Paddy Considine, it's a summation of life as a British adolescent and gained a cult following, with Turner's songs fittingly capturing the emotion-fuelled travails of the lead characters, accompanying keys moments in the lead protagonist's emotional journey.

It was a perfect fit, as Ayoade well knew. The sort of untampered desire that can only be found in youth was Alex Turner's stock-in-trade and the soundtrack highlights it perfectly. Hiding Tonight sees the narrator dreaming of a better mood and better days ('Tomorrow I'll be stronger, running colourful, no longer just in black and white,') while on Glass in The Park he's passionately protecting his love, whether she wants him to or not ('If the sun's in your eyes, I'll tighten the blindfold, baby,').

On It's Hard to Get Around the Wind he's chasing the unattainable ('Even when you know the way it's gonna blow, it's hard to get around the wind,') while the puzzle (Stuck on The Puzzle) is the eternal difference between men and women, which he freely admits he cannot solve. A strong set of wistfully romantic songs, with the strongest (Piledriver Waltz) so good that Turner submitted it for the next Arctic Monkeys album.

Films had always been a keen interest of Turner's, but when asked if *Submarine* would be the first of many by BBC 6Music, the singer was cagey: 'Not necessarily. I don't think of this as a soundtrack. I just wrote a few tunes and they happened to fit. I don't think I'd be very good at doing the soundtrack for *Transformers* or anything like that.' However, when asked if he'd be interested in a James Bond theme, he replied, 'Well, that's a different story. I'd love to do a tune for Bond. Definitely.'(xlviii)

Alex Turner – *Submarine* EP

Released: 14th March 2011; UK Chart Position: 35;
Label: Domino
Track Listing: Stuck on The Puzzle (Intro); Hiding Tonight; Glass in The Park; It's Hard to Get Around the Wind; Stuck on The Puzzle; Piledriver Waltz
Producer: James Ford
All lyrics by Alex Turner; all music by Alex Turner and James Ford

Turner did another favour for a different friend in co-writing a hefty six songs for fellow Last Shadow Puppet Miles Kane's debut solo album *Colour of The Trap,* released in May 2011. Credited along with Kane, Turner's name was put to the single Rearrange, album tracks Counting Down the Days, Happenstance (which featured a guest appearance from French actor Clémence Poésy), Telepathy, Better Left Invisible, and the title track, which also included Andy Sweeney as a writer. Flexing his powerful address book, Kane was able to call in indie heavyweights Gruff Rhys and Noel Gallagher to contribute to the album.

None of these projects came at the expense of his band with Turner spending 2010 writing new material, later telling *Metro* magazine: 'I wrote a lot of the new album while I was living in New York and I found myself using more English colloquialisms than ever,'(xlix) (Turner having relocated to Brooklyn with his girlfriend).

During this period of writing, he was making a conscious effort to write in major keys, perhaps affected by the more 'classic' song writing style more prevalent across the Atlantic. In addition, his speaking voice had taken an American inflection; slower and deeper with his Yorkshire accent less pronounced (for which he would take some mockery), perhaps inevitably because of his new surroundings, and he displayed a more laid-back, confident approach in interviews.

In the autumn, Turner was joined in America by Jamie Cook to add guitar parts to the songs written so far, before reconvening the rest of the band to finesse their workings. James Ford, the last addition to the process, proposed that the group develop the new songs to a point that they would be ready to record quickly, and so the band spent several months rehearsing but not putting anything to tape

This new approach saw the announcement of James Ford as the producer for their fourth album in January 2011, before the recording had been concluded. The sessions took place at the legendary Sound City Studios in Los Angeles, using live takes with minimal overdubbing, which according to Turner meant, 'we could really concentrate on beefing up the guitar sounds.'(1)

In readiness for their fourth album, Arctic Monkeys announced two homecoming gigs at Sheffield Don Valley Bowl in early June. Then, a few days before the release of *Submarine*, the title of the new album was announced (*Suck It and See*) alongside a 'taster' song: Brick by Brick. A big, dumb, simple rock song with lead vocals from Matt Helders (the chorus sung by Turner), it came complete with a video set in LA with shots of the band on a beach in California, along with a woman playing a record of the song in her apartment.

In an interview with *NME*, Helders provided some details of the sound of the new album: 'Some of the songs are a bit more instant. A bit more poppy, certainly than *Humbug* was. It's enjoyable for us and the listener. And it's maybe a bit more easy-going. Not easy listening, but with a few poppier tunes. But in an interesting way.'(li)

In a separate interview, also with *NME,* Alex Turner laid down a gauntlet in the hope that another aspiring guitar band would pick it up: 'Everyone thinks that the next big thing has got to sound really modern and new, but to get something that sounds fresh, it can just be three kids with guitars and not a lot else. There's enough username-and-password music already, know what I mean? I hope it does happen again, though. Because we'll never get that initial naivety back...you can't, like, fake that thing, like what's on the first record. It's just a time and a place...but yeah, I'd love for a band to come through and turn the charts upside down for a couple of weeks.'(lii) Sadly, at the time of writing (2022), the wait for a guitar band to storm the charts goes on. He also revealed that he and his bandmates had been listening to Nick Cave, John Cale, Lou Reed, Leonard Cohen, and David Bowie, hoping for motivation to write better-crafted songs.

Brick by Brick worked as a tease for the album and was included on the first official single release in April 2011. Don't Sit Down 'Cause I've Moved Your Chair features basic guitar chords before Turner's vocals strike out as if singing from across a canyon, preceding a monstrous, pounding riff crashing in alongside bass and drums. A simple chorus of 'yeah yeah yeah' and a huge drop do the job effectively if basically, the band rowing back on the over-complications of *Humbug.* It's full of British references ('wear your shell suit on Bonfire Night,') that sit strangely but comfortably against the massive soundscape and, to emphasise the points, Alex Turner would perform actions to the lyrics on the stage.

Speaking with *NME*, Turner explained the story behind the lyrics: 'That's something (the title) someone said. In fact, I said it to somebody whose chair I moved and I didn't want them to hurt themselves. That was while we were in the studio doing the *Submarine* recording and James (Ford) said, 'Oh, that sounds like it could be '60s garage *Nuggets* tune and be called that'. So then we thought, 'Well, OK, if that's what you can't do, then what sort of ridiculous things can you do that are probably more dangerous than if you just sat down?' (liii)

Single 11:

Don't Sit Down 'Cause I've Moved Your Chair
Released: 16th April 2011; UK Chart Position: 28;
Label: Domino; Album: *Suck It and See*
B-Sides: Brick by Brick; I.D.S.T.; The Blond-O-Sonic Shimmer Trap
Producer: James Ford
All songs written by Alex Turner except Brick by Brick (Turner/Helders)

While basic, Brick by Brick's lyrics could be seen as a manifesto for the new approach: 'I wanna build you up, I wanna break you down, I'm gonna reconstruct,' although that may be giving it more credit than its worth. Intending to go back to basics, which may well have applied also to the lyrics (in this case), it was the result of a challenge the band had set themselves to write a song with less than 20 words.

Almost a riposte to critics who had found

Humbug too challenging, it's a big, dumb, nonsense slice of surf-rock, fun if nothing else although, ironically, its simplicity was initially underwhelming. Certainly, I.D.S.T. (short for If Destroyed Still True, a popular mantra), also sung by Helders, sustains the theme, though it is snappier and more purposeful than Brick by Brick. Similarly, The Blond-O-Sonic Shimmer Trap rattles and jerks both anxiously and confidently.

The video for Don't Sit Down 'Cause I've Moved Your Chair was largely a performance video shot through an old video camera with vast amounts of distortion and colour, interspersed with images of the band in a Cadillac, clips of Sheffield Wednesday in various football matches and an old computer showing the word 'Don't', matching the single's artwork.

UK Singles Chart – Top 10 – 23rd April 2011:

1. Party Rock Anthem – LMFAO/Lauren Bennett/Goonrock
2. On The Floor – Jennifer Lopez ft Pitbull
3. ET – Katy Perry ft Kanye West
4. Sweat – Snoop Dogg
5. Just Can't Get Enough – Black Eyed Peas
6. Someone Like You – Adele
7. S&M – Rihanna
8. Beautiful People – Chris Brown ft Benny Benassi
9. Buzzin – Man ft 50 Cent
10. Don't Hold Your Breath – Nicole Scherzinger

……………………………………………………………

28. Don't Sit Down 'Cause I've Moved Your Chair – Arctic Monkeys

In a lengthy interview with *Sound on Sound,* James Ford shed some light on the recording process for the forthcoming album. 'They've never been fans of big, fancy, all-singing, all-dancing studios,' said the producer. 'So it's more about trying to find a place that's got a bit of a vibe that they can relax into. They don't really like the kind of studio where you press a button and the walls move. It has to be a bit more real,' he explained. 'They'd all be facing Matt, playing live. Sometimes we had amps in the room, sometimes the amps were in iso booths.'

Detailing the live recording process, Ford continued: 'Quite a lot of the time we ended up going over the vocal, but something like Library Pictures is the vocal from the actual live take...pretty much what we heard is what you get.'(liv)

Elsewhere on the press rounds to launch *Suck It and See,* Alex Turner revealed the group mentality for the new album: 'The main thing I learned is that whatever it is that makes us sound like us is built into the four of us,' he told *The Observer.* In the same interview, he dismissed the notion that he was the voice of a generation: 'I just don't think I'm equipped to soundtrack the times. There might be someone out there who can do that, but I haven't cracked it.'(lv)

Back on the road, the group played their first live shows for the tour in May 2011, with two sets in Scandinavia where they debuted four of the album's songs, while the UK comeback launched with a special guest slot at the Radio 1 *Big Weekend* in Carlisle as they opened the two-day event with a 12-song set. A few days later, speaking to the station's DJ Zane Lowe, the frontman explained how he viewed the upcoming set of songs: 'I think the new album is a balance between our first three. There's nothing about taxi ranks or anything like that, but there's a bit of a standpoint I had on those early songs and the sense of humour, but there's also a bit of the *Humbug* stuff which is kind of off in the corners.'(lvi)

In the days leading up to its release, it was revealed that *Suck It and See* was to be censored in large American supermarkets. The senior management teams deemed the title to be too provocative for family consumption, with the cover a stark yellow image simply bearing the title and nothing else. Being a resident of the US, Turner must have known this would be a possibility, but all involved apparently concluded that the adage of 'no such thing as bad press' made it a risk worth taking.

Album 4:

Suck It and See
Released: 6th June 2011; UK Chart Position: 1; Label: Domino
Track Listing: She's Thunderstorms; Black Treacle; Brick by Brick; The Hellcat Spangled Shalalala; Don't Sit Down 'Cause I've Moved Your Chair; Library Pictures; All My Own Stunts; Reckless Serenade; Piledriver Waltz; Love Is a Laserquest; Suck It And See; That's Where You're Wrong
Producer: James Ford
All songs written by Alex Turner except Brick by Brick (Turner/Helders)

From the very outset, aside from a brief prickly riff to open proceedings, *Suck It and See* is a lighter album than *Humbug.* The opening track, She's Thunderstorms, (ironically) lets the sunshine in after the previous dusky sounds, the verse carrying a sheen that radiates positivity. The keys frequently change but Nick O'Malley's basslines match them accordingly, while Jamie Cook provides a strangled, off-piste psychedelic solo. Thunderstorms (plural) is a new way Turner finds of complimenting a person; she's not just one, she's many, as the girl in question gives him 'this kind of acrobatic blood concertina, cheating heart-beat, rapid-fire.'

More weather references abound on Black Treacle, as ‘the sky looks sticky’ while he doesn’t ‘mean to rain on anybody’s Cabriolet.’ The song has a strange construction with a gloopy, unhurried start, as Turner casts doubt over a romantic situation (‘one of those games you’re gonna lose but you wanna play it just in case,’) which gives way to a hurried end, as he reflects that he may be feeling the ravages of time. ‘I’m out of place and I’m not getting any wiser, I feel like the Sundance Kid behind a synthesizer,’ he ruminates, knowing that the situation is doomed, accompanied by a nonchalant, despondent riff. The narcotic illusions referenced also suggest a recent familiarity with marijuana.

Brick by Brick lightens the mood and somehow still manages to cram in a love reference (‘I wanna feel your love,’) before The Hellcat Spangled Shalalala elevates things to a more ecstatic plane, if only musically. A superb bassline works in conjunction with a dreamy, jangly riff, echoing down the fretboard in the vein of Johnny Marr while also screeching intermittently. Like the previous single, the chorus is devoid of lyrics, possibly down to the group wanting to keep things basic (but catchy) with a middle eight, something not often deployed by the band.

The lyrics, however, tell a different story as, ‘things are getting complicated in the eye of the storm,’ as the hellcat in question has ‘flicked a red-hot revelation off the tip of her tongue,' namely cut deep in the heat of an argument. The protagonist is aware that going 'home sweet home,' is a 'booby trap' and that 'these are things she's said before,' so all they can do is throw it to the wind and sing (shalalala).

When speaking of the album as an amalgamation of the previous three, one can assume that Turner was thinking of the next two songs. Library Pictures is structurally like the tracks on *Humbug* and much heavier than those around it, giving Matt Helders the chance to spread his wings for the first time. Lyrically abstract, though possibly sexual, Turner hides his process in plain sight 'through curly straws and metaphors and goo.'

Similar in vibe, All My Own Stunts (featuring Josh Homme on backing vocals) has a moody verse with a sparkling chorus and allows the band to wig out with incessant drums and a rickety guitar sound. Turner's love of the cinema comes into play once again, both in the title and as he informs that he's 'been watching cowboy films on gloomy afternoons.' Their first album gets a nod as he asks the girl to 'put on your dancing shoes' as 'sorrow slow dances around the edges of her eyes.'

With those two tracks placed next to one another, and the following four similar in tone, the sequencing of the album seems a bit odd, unless we are in the middle of another narrative which, given how in-depth Alex Turner can be, would be foolish to discount. Reckless Serenade is probably the most inessential song on the album, although it still glistens and features the wonderful line, 'Called up to listen to the voice of reason and got his answering machine,' as Turner ponders on his life as a songwriter, 'singing a reckless serenade.'

Piledriver Waltz is given the full band

treatment as opposed to the simpler, acoustic version on *Submarine*, and the debate as to which version is better rages on years later. The earlier version was in the key of C-Sharp while presented here in E, yet the change doesn't affect the sluggish, despondent mood, while the ear-piercing electric guitar emphasises the vibe better. For once the lyrics are unambiguous but the quality of the poetry remains, the narrator resigned to being dumped as the focus of the song has 'been for breakfast at the Heartbreak Hotel,' as he's heard that, 'you're planning to shoot me out of a cannon.' He can't resist a slight at her but even then, he wishes her well: 'If you're gonna try and walk on water, make sure you wear your comfortable shoes.'

Similar in theme and pace, Love Is a Laserquest finds the narrator reflecting on a relationship from some distance with some of Alex Turner's most universal and accurate lyrics, the influence of Leonard Cohen shining through. 'I've tried to ask you this in some daydreams that I've had but you're always busy being make-believe,' is as heart-breaking a lyric as he's written, and concludes on an equally poignant note: 'Will I have found a better method of pretending you were just some lover', as a mournful guitar illuminates the song's ending.

The title track (the first time Arctic Monkeys had done so) finds Turner thinking more optimistically, imploring a girl to take a chance (i.e., the title) while he both self-deprecates then shows off on the wondrous second verse: 'I poured my aching heart into a pop song, I couldn't get the hang of poetry. That's not a skirt girl, that's a sawn-off shotgun and I can only hope you've got it aimed at me.' The guitar evokes an almost 1950s sound with a splendid solo while the trundling bass garners a righteous, hopeful feel. With an earworm of a melody, it's little wonder it was chosen as a single.

For once, the lyrics are outdone by the musicianship on the divine That's Where You're Wrong, the band keeping things simple through the prism of classic indie outfits such as The Cure and The Smiths while aiming directly for the heart. O'Malley's descending bassline drives the song forward toward the defiant outro, as does the dazzling guitar motif. For once, the narrator is in control as he informs the woman, almost cruelly, that, 'you're not the only one that time has got it in for honey, that's where you're wrong,' as she is but one of many 'old flames fastened on.' A rare example of an unheralded Arctic Monkeys song and a glorious way to finish a fine album which also promises a brighter future.

Suck It and See maintains the heft of the previous album but is consciously chiselled to sound lighter and fresher, not least with more obvious choruses. There is less of a discernible theme than on previous albums, although certain lyrical reference points infrequently pop up, such as the weather, or archaic British terminologies such as dandelion and burdock, treacle, and laser quest. It can't be a coincidence that the title sits nicely alongside the previous album's boiled sweet, but it could also be the band encouraging listeners to give them another try. It's a stretch to connect it to the weather theme but it could be the action of wetting one's finger to assess the wind's direction.

It must be said that it's quite safe in comparison to the previous risky move and the band may have been over-compensating to please their audience with its consciously cheery songs. They admitted limiting themselves in their determination to write traditional numbers, although the return of the humour and warmth is welcome. The most striking element of the album is the directness of Turner's lyrics; although still drowning in endlessly quotable metaphors, he takes the first person, perhaps sometimes as a character, sometimes not. Either way, it cruises lightly down the highway as the sun comes up, the dawn after the night before.

Reviews for *Suck It and See* were broadly positive, as if the music press were relieved that they didn't have to be challenged quite so readily again. True to form, the *NME* sang its praises loudest, declaring that 'the band know exactly where they're going. Four albums in, and they've yet to shed so much as an ounce of purpose or inspiration,' and declared that 'they've aced it, well and truly'(lvii) although notoriously hard-to-please website *The Quietus* felt that it 'hits more than it misses (just),' but ultimately concluded that Turner and co were still 'one of our most interesting and frequently brilliant pop bands.'(lviii)

The Guardian oddly declared *Suck It and See* as 'the first Arctic Monkeys album that tries to ensnare the listener with its tunes, rather than guitar riffs or Turner's lyrics,' and that its 'worst crime isn't overindulgence, but occasionally sounding ordinary,'(lix) although it was still deemed worthy of 4 stars. Even former cynics *Pitchfork* were coming round to the band (albeit only with a 7.5 score), noting that 'the record itself brims with endlessly replayable details, some goofy and some poignant, both in frontman Alex Turner's always keenly observed lyrics and the band's ever-proficient musicianship, the latter of which ranges here from muscular glam-rock to chiming indie pop balladry.'(lx)

The album's release was the first milestone in a big week for the band, as they hosted two homecoming shows at the Don Valley Bowl in Sheffield, under a specially made big-top tent. With support from Dead Sons, Mabel Love, Anna Calvi, The Vaccines, and their old friend Miles Kane (who joined them for 505), Arctic Monkeys left 20,000 fans (split across both nights) in raptures with several older songs reintroduced to the set, including the first outing for Mardy Bum in four years, yet the crowd sang along equally as loudly to the newer tracks. A trailer for the shows, indicating a DVD version, was released later in the year but has yet to see the light of day.

<u>The setlist was:</u>

The View from The Afternoon
Brianstorm
This House Is a Circus
Still Take You Home
Don't Sit Down 'Cause I've Moved Your Chair
Library Pictures
Teddy Picker
Crying Lightning
Brick by Brick
The Hellcat Spangled Shalalala
Cornerstone
Mardy Bum
I Bet You Look Good on The Dancefloor
She's Thunderstorms
Pretty Visitors
If You Were There, Beware
Do Me A Favour
That's Where You're Wrong
505

When The Sun Goes Down
Fluorescent Adolescent
A Certain Romance

As was becoming tradition, on the day after the second show Arctic Monkeys had another reason to celebrate as *Suck It and See* went straight to the top of the UK Album Chart. More impressive was that it succeeded where other guitar heavyweights had failed in 2011. Elbow, The Strokes, Radiohead, and Liam Gallagher's new outfit Beady Eye had all fallen at the feet of Adele's second album *21* which had, at this point, spent 15 weeks at the top before being usurped by Lady Gaga with *Born This Way*. The boys from Sheffield held them both at bay if only for a week, becoming only the second band to have four consecutive Number 1 albums (although the other was Keane, lessening the achievement).

<u>UK Album Chart – Top 10 – 12th June 2011:</u>

1. ***Suck It and See* – Arctic Monkeys**
2. *21* – Adele
3. *Born This Way* – Lada Gaga
4. *Dream With Me* – Jackie Evancho
5. *19* – Adele
6. *Glee – The Music – Vol 6* – Glee Cast
7. *You Can't Teach an Old Dog New Tricks* – Seasick Steve
8. *Wonderland* – Wonderland
9. *Who You Are* – Jessie J
10. *Doo-Wops and Hooligans* – Bruno Mars

One question rarely asked of the group was how long they planned to continue, as it would surely be difficult to sustain the same levels of success, especially considering two members had already dipped their toe into other projects. However, when speaking to *Spin,* the group revealed it wasn't a question they had asked themselves either. 'We really have got no plan at all about how many records or how long we'll go,' answered Nick O'Malley while Turner, when asked if they saw other bands as role models, replied: 'They all end up hating each other, don't they? I can't imagine being in me 60s playing. I'll try to keep the boots on as long as I can. I'm saying that now, who knows how I'll feel?'(lxi)

CHAPTER NINE
'I Poured My Aching Heart Into A Pop Song' (2011-2013)

Another busy summer of festivals lay before Arctic Monkeys in 2011, although when Alex Turner was seen at Glastonbury the rumour mill went into overdrive until he confirmed his presence was just as an attendee. After a run across Europe, they played the iTunes Festival and T in the Park, their second headline set after being the festival's first Friday headliners in 2007. Six of the tracks performed at the former were released as a special, iTunes-only EP: Brianstorm, Don't Sit Down 'Cause I've Moved Your Chair, Crying Lightning, The Hellcat Spangled Shalalala, I Bet You Look Good on The Dancefloor, and 505.

In early August they embarked on an American tour, during which Turner underwent a complete change of haircut, replacing his regulation indie-mod style with a slicked-back, teddy-boy quiff to go with his tight t-shirt and leather jacket. Jamie Cook had already adopted a smarter, side-parting style and, while superficial, it seemed to herald a new attitude from Turner in particular, who had become notably more confident and gregarious in his stage manner in the vein of a 'traditional' (if cliched) rock star. Many rock stars would emulate the hairstyle over the preceding years, including Kasabian's Tom Meighan and Liam Fray from Courteeners.

As the group was warming up for their slot at Lollapalooza in Chicago, back in the UK there was trouble brewing on the streets of London. A protest and vigil were taking place in Tottenham to mark the death of Mark Duggan, a young man who had been shot dead by the Metropolitan Police. The vigil turned violent, with police cars attacked by youths. In the days that followed, the disturbances spread across London and other cities in the UK including the looting of shops and other commercial properties, causing an estimated £200 million worth of property damage as well as a handful of deaths.

One of the buildings almost completely wiped out was Sony's CD manufacturing warehouse in Enfield where (as well as the major label) countless other independent labels' physical products were stored. Millions of independent records were destroyed, including virtually the entire stock of the next Arctic Monkeys single, The Hellcat Spangled Shalalala.

The band was forced to cancel the release, although some vinyl copies of the record were salvaged and made available the following week. A few weeks later, Alex Turner had his say on the events, telling *Uncut:* 'The thing is that, even if you buy what the papers are saying and assume everyone involved is just some mindless thug or whatever they're calling them, I think we still need to ask why this country has produced so many mindless thugs.'

'I mean you can't just treat this thing as if it was entirely unrelated to anything else. If all these kids are hooligans and thieves, then why are they all hooligans and thieves?'(lxii) A valid question, still yet to be answered. Meanwhile, the video, directed by Focus Creeps, featured images of the band on the road and in LA along with snippets of model Scarlett Kapella as the 'hellcat' (wearing a catsuit, naturally).

The solitary B-side, unrestrained rocker Little Illusion Machine (Wirral Riddler), was credited to The Death Ramps and Miles Kane (who appeared onstage with the band regularly throughout the summer) with the latter on lead vocals for the entire song (barring one verse which Turner sang). The dual factors of the song being in the public domain for two months and the lack of physical product meant the song barely scraped into the top 200.

<u>Single 12:</u>

The Hellcat Spangled Shalalala
Released: 15th August 2011; UK Chart Position: N/A; Label: Domino; Album: *Suck It and See*
B-Side: Little Illusion Machine (Wirral Riddler)
Producer: James Ford and Ross Orton
Little Illusion (Wirral Riddler) written by Arctic Monkeys/Miles Kane

In other news, it had been speculated that, as their deal with Domino was due to expire, the availability of the group could spark a bidding war between major labels. However, it came to naught as the group stayed with the independent label, no doubt aware that the creative leeway offered to them may have been curtailed were they to move elsewhere.

With a maiden appearance at the V Festival on the horizon, the band spoke to *Shortlist* about a wide variety of subjects, including the state of guitar music. When asked if he agreed with Liam Gallagher that the genre was in a rut, Turner was pleasingly righteous: 'Definitely. But that's all the more reason for us to play at V Festival and be right in the middle of all that. It will come back around. People ask us why we released Don't Sit Down...as the first single, because it's not the poppiest one on there – it's really guitar-heavy. But because we've got that fanbase and we're one of the guitar bands that have a shot of getting on the radio in the daytime, I almost feel like it's our job to put that sort of tune out.'

'When you talk about pop music dominating,' he continued, 'it's not like it's all shit and we're dead against it. That's not the case at all, because there are some great pop songs. Some of it is nonsense, but it's not like we're completely trying to destroy it. And if we do V Festival we can get right into the nucleus.'(lxiii) For what it was worth, the V Festival sets went down well, even if the crowds were there for the other headliner (Rihanna).

In other interviews in the same period, Turner revealed that the band was looking to take a break and he had no other projects to focus on. 'I've kind of put a record out every year in some way, shape, or form,' he told the *Toronto Sun,* 'But for the first time, there's nothing in the works. I've got no plans. We're just enjoying being on tour. And that's what we're focusing on now – to be honest, that's all we're focusing on. We're not even thinking about the next album.'(lxiv)

With the perpetually evolving sound and having played certain songs for several years, specifically I Bet You Look Good on The Dancefloor, it would be understandable if the group were bored of playing the older material. However, Alex Turner felt differently when speaking to *NME*, also revealing a surprising bit of information about the song's gestation: 'It's more fun than ever to play it now. I probably fell out with it for a moment somewhere along the way. But I fall out with all of them at some point,' he told the magazine. 'I'd never imagine not playing, and now when it comes round in the set it's just like...fun. We all really enjoy playing that.'

'It's funny, because when we were recording that tune, the video was already on telly for it. So people would be watching TV in the other room or whatever and be like, 'Quick! We're on *MTV* or whatever, because the version we did for the video we did another recording for it, it was just us playing in a TV studio.'

'It all came from that drum thing at the beginning originally. That was the first part of the song, that drum bit. I play the lead on it, but I really can't remember when that happened, or even what practice room we were in. But I remember Matt playing that thing. I guess it was some exercise that he'd seen somewhere or a version of it, which he'd sped up because he was going at it as fast as he could. A lot of those songs back then came from something that he'd played, because he almost plays riffs on drums, or plays leads.'(lxv)

In a separate interview with BBC 6Music, Turner discussed his new performative approach on stage: 'I have started to enjoy that side of things and I've done things on stage recently that I never thought I would have done. Being up there in the limelight, if you like, is something that didn't come naturally to me, like singing, it's something that has built up over time. But now I'm doing stupid crowd participation things like shouting, 'just this side sing.' That was a gag that we used to have in the practice room but I actually went through with it the other night and I felt like I had to apologise.'(xlvi)

Lastly, when asked by *GQ* magazine if he had any ambitions left, the frontman revealed that a certain headline slot was an itch still to be scratched: 'I'd really like another shot at headlining Glastonbury. I don't think we got that quite right when we did it.'(lxvii) Meanwhile, despite his band touring Europe and the US in the autumn of 2011, Matt Helders found the time to work on another remix: the Wet Nuns track Heaven Below.

The excessive touring of the United States was starting to pay off, with larger venues being filled. Turner noted as much: 'We're in a good place. Just coming to the end of this American tour, but it's been really good. America has really started to like us. We've started getting a really good response.'(lxviii) Tellingly, in line with Turner's comments, the video for the next single (Suck It and See) was shot in America and told a narrative story of a biker (played by Matt Helders, who had recently bought a motorbike himself) and his relationship with his lover, played by American model Breana McDow.

Inspired by the film *Badlands* (and set in California), it mocked the macho nature of American biker culture and was the first of three videos (all directed by Focus Creeps) centred around the character, the storyline continuing in the video for B-side Evil Twin, itself a Motorhead-inspired, dusky rock number. The single was released in conjunction with the UK arena tour.

Single 13:

Suck It and See
Released: 31st October 2011; UK Chart Position: 149; Label: Domino; Album: *Suck It and See*
B-Side: Evil Twin
Producer: James Ford

Following current trends, with the single available as a download for several months, Evil Twin charted higher (114) than Suck It and See (149) on the UK Singles Chart. Helders threw himself into the role for the video, dressed in a sleeveless denim jacket (with the name of the song in the style of a biker group on the back) and leather trousers (his own). The drummer later commented on the unusual video to *NME*: 'It's a strange thing to do, isn't it? Was I worried that people might not get the joke? I wasn't that bothered as long as people see that we don't take ourselves too seriously.'

2012 began with a flurry of Arctic Monkeys activity including a tour of Australia and New Zealand, the announcement of an appearance at the Coachella Festival in California (part of a wider US tour supporting The Black Keys) and, surprisingly given Turner's previous comments, plans for a new EP. In addition, they performed a cover of Katy B's On A Mission for Radio 1's *Live Lounge* as part of the promotional activity for the fourth and last single from *Suck It And See.* Ross Orton, from electroclash outfit Fat Truckers, produced the B-side.

Single 14:

Black Treacle
Released: 23rd January 2012; UK Chart Position: N/A; Label: Domino; Album: *Suck It and See*
B-Side: You and I
Producer: James Ford and Ross Orton
You and I written by Cook/Hawley/Helders/O'Malley/Turner

The video, the last part of the biker saga, saw Helders' character in prison before escaping and running to meet his bride at a location in the desert.

In stark contrast, You and I's video featured Turner and Helders on their motorbikes driving around Sheffield, accompanying Jamie Cook and Nick O'Malley in a classic sports car, as well as studio images with Richard Hawley. Another song credited to The Death Ramps, Hawley provided a growling vocal and spindly guitar solo for the B-side.

In February, two days before picking up another *NME* award for Best Live Band (the only gong they picked up from seven nominations), Arctic Monkeys released a brand-new single. The release of R U Mine? was surely both the shortest time ever between the releases of the last single from one album and the first single from the next, as well as the longest lead time between the single and album. However, it should be noted that the original intention was for the song to be a one-off, with a special physical release for Record Store Day in April.

Single 15:

R U Mine?
Released: 27th February 2012; UK Chart Position: 23; Label: Domino; Album: *AM*
B-Side: Electricity
Producer: Ross Orton
R U Mine? written by Alex Turner and Nick O'Malley

Like a cavalcade of rock explosions, RU Mine? heralded yet another new era for Arctic Monkeys. A moment of inspiration lead to the bravura riff by Nick O'Malley, who also contributes a bulging bassline and high-pitched backing vocals which sparked a new lease of life from Matt Helders (not that one was needed). Equally impressed was Alex Turner, who delivers a swaggering vocal to complement his new stage persona. In contrast, he murmurs on Electricity, almost reluctant to compete with the rollicking riff and guitar lick that aurally represents the title. Both tracks ooze Queens of The Stone Age-esque sleaze and surprisingly only bagged an underwhelming number 23 on the UK Singles chart.

UK Singles Chart – Top 10 - 4th March 2012:

1. Somebody That I Used to Know – Gotye ft Kimbra
2. Rockstar – Dappy ft Brian May
3. Next To Me – Emeli Sande
4. Wild Ones – Flo Rida ft Sia
5. Starships – Nicki Minaj
6. Hot Right Now – DJ Fresh ft Rita Ora
7. Titanium – David Guetta ft Sia
8. Stronger – Kelly Clarkson
9. Drunk – Ed Sheeran
10. Domino – Jessie J

....

23. R U Mine? – Arctic Monkeys

Speaking with the *NME* post-release, Turner was uncharacteristically thorough when explaining the song's meaning and content: 'There's a few references for people to pick up on in there – Some Velvet Morning, Tracy Island. Those references are just me being a smart-arse. The song, not to get too heavy, is about that uncertainty that comes with love sometimes. Wonder where you are with it all. That's the undertone for the tune, but I threw in a *Thunderbirds* reference too. Just because.'

In the same piece, Turner revealed his latest

song-writing inspirations. 'That particular bit is like the thing Lil Wayne and Drake do. We've been listening to a lot of their stuff recently. I like that thing they do where they talk about something backwards, so they talk about it but then say what it actually is on the next line. It's hard to explain but I guess it's a little nod to that idea. So I say, 'I'm a puppet on a string,' just before mentioning Tracy Island. That's what it's about – uncertainty.'(lxix)

The video, once again directed by Focus Creeps, featured an appearance by former Sex Pistols guitarist Steve Jones, debuting the song on his show on American modern rock radio station KROQ-FM. One long sequence, it showed Turner, Helders, and O'Malley lip-syncing the song in a car, with Cook represented by an image on a TV. Speaking of the video to *Paste* magazine, Helders explained the concept: 'This idea was sometimes when we're messing around driving we film ourselves singing stupid songs on the radio, people do that I think, and in a way we wanted to do a video we could put out straight away without any promotion, which is what we did with Brick by Brick.'

'We didn't tell anybody we were releasing it, we just put it out. In a way, that worked better than any other video we've put out. And R U Mine?, more people have watched it than any other video on this album. So obviously it worked.'(lxx) In the same piece, Helders confirmed that the song would be standalone, in conjunction with their support slot (their first and, to date, only) with The Black Keys.

Speaking to the *Examiner,* the drummer explained their unusual decision to be a support band, eight years into their career: 'We've been looking for a tour like this since we started because we've never done a support tour, not in England, not anywhere. We were trying to think what the right band would be, and we had some good offers that didn't work out, timing-wise, from other bands. For this (tour) we thought it would be stupid to turn it down. It's a massive tour, and I think we've done as much as we could on our own without doing something like this.'

Helders also went on to explain that the group saw themselves playing faster songs for the near future: 'The way R U Mine? has gone we are more into doing songs like that for now. We are kind of into the idea of doing a record that is like Evil Twin and R U Mine?'(lxxi) Nick O'Malley reiterated the stance speaking with *Spinner* when asked about their fifth album: 'It's quite early days yet. We've not really got any songs for it at all, so it's difficult to say what the album will be like. But we're enjoying playing sort of fast songs at the minute, so maybe that'll be an indication that it may go that way.'(lxxii) In a separate interview with *Artrocker,* Turner confirmed as much: 'I think we're going to go in the direction of those heavier tunes.'

'We feel the strength of the last record is Don't Sit Down...the other songs like that – Brick By Brick – the other side of it is fine, but I don't know how much more of that we can do.'(lxxiv) As the tour progressed and the interviews continued, Matt Helders explained the group's overall attitude to their career to *The Calgary Herald*: 'We've never really thought that we can let expectation dictate what kind of music we make. I think it's important we make a record that we think is good and hopefully people share that opinion. Since that first record, we've all changed, and hopefully, the people that we into us have changed as well, grown up with us.'(lxxiii) Meanwhile, Alex Turner's latest collaboration with

Miles Kane was released in April 2012, as a co-writer on the one-off single First of My Kind, while Helders' remix of the title track from Paul Weller's album *That Dangerous Age* debuted a month earlier.

In the UK, the imminent Olympics (taking place in London) dominated the summer of 2012. There was much speculation about the opening ceremony, traditionally a celebration of the culture of the host nation. Director Danny Boyle, best known for pioneering films such as *Shallow Grave, Trainspotting, Sunshine,* and *Slumdog Millionaire* was responsible for directing the opening spectacle, but the contents were kept a closely guarded secret.

The over-arching theme for the four-hour event, entitled *Isles of Wonder,* was a celebration of Britishness divided into three principal movements: a transition from Green and Pleasant Land to the Pandemonium of the industrial revolution, a salute to the NHS and children's literature, and a celebration of pop-culture, technology, and the digital revolution. The night was full of surprises, most notably a short film about James Bond (as played by Daniel Craig) and the Queen which culminated in 'the pair' parachuting into the brand-new Olympic Stadium in Stratford, East London.

After the Parade of Nations (the sequence of the opening ceremony in which every competing athlete would be introduced to the stadium as part of their country's team), was concluded, a grinding guitar and drums blared out from the sound system. At one end of the dazzlingly lit stadium were Arctic Monkeys tearing into I Bet You Look Good on The Dancefloor, with Alex Turner wearing his now-trademark leather jacket and Matt Helders in a GB tracksuit (complete with his surname on the back) playing a drumkit emblazoned with the United

Kingdom's national flag. Accompanied by a breath-taking firework display, the group threw themselves into their debut single with gusto, before lowering the temperature with a faithful cover of The Beatles' Come Together, as 75 cyclists emerged from beneath the band's platform to circle the stadium with wings lit by LED to represent doves of peace.

Although their appearance, as one of only a handful of performances (alongside Dizzee Rascal, Mike Oldfield, Emeli Sande, and Paul McCartney) during the ceremony, was a surprise, as the UK's foremost rock band Arctic Monkeys were a logical choice. The event, which Turner and company took two months out from recording to coordinate, was about celebrating Great Britain's historical and contemporary culture, and no other band could compete with the foursome in terms of contemporary mainstream success. With a worldwide audience of over 27 million people, the group also had the most important slot just before McCartney, bookending the history of British rock music.

The Olympic ceremony's soundtrack album, *Isles of Wonder*, was released digitally at midnight on 28th July. Mostly pre-recorded, the two contributions from Arctic Monkeys were credited in the album sleeve as being recorded during the rehearsal at the stadium on 23 July 2012. While not officially a single, Come Together still reached an impressive number 21 on the UK Singles Chart in the week after its release, while I Bet You Look Good on The Dancefloor re-entered at number 78.

Stand Alone Single:

Come Together (Lennon/McCartney)
Released: 28th July 2012: UK Chart Position: 21;

Label: Decca; Album: *Isles of Wonder*

UK Singles Chart – Top 10 – 5th August 2012:

1. Heatwave – Wiley ft MS D
2. We'll Be Coming Back – Calvin Harris ft Example
3. Spectrum – Florence & The Machine
4. Payphone – Maroon 5 ft Wiz Khalifa
5. Black Heart – Stooshe
6. Brokenhearted – Karmin
7. Feel The Love – Rudimental ft John Newman
8. Don't Wake Me Up – Chris Brown
9. Vegas Girl – Conor Maynard
10. Whistle – Flo Rida

....

21. Come Together – Arctic Monkeys

One year on from the ceremony, Alex Turner revealed that their appearance at the extravaganza had caused some understandable nerves: 'We did the Olympics thing last year and I was really nervous. Until about 10 seconds before I walked out, I was like, 'What is happening here?! I was in a weird panic. We never had fireworks until we did that Olympics thing – we didn't know what was happening. It was great, man. You can't lose, you can do anything if you have fireworks!'(lxxv) Elsewhere, when speaking to the *NME* as part of the magazine's 60th-anniversary celebrations, Turner named John Lennon as his ultimate icon and discussed his thoughts about their recent cover.

'Come Together, which we just played at the Olympics – I found that song difficult to get anywhere near. I've heard that song a thousand times before, but there's not one word in that song that logically leads into the next one. It's all a jumble, but it's not just that, if you know what I mean. It paints you a picture and puts you in this place. He's got a way of leading you somewhere with these unusual words that don't make sense, but also make perfect fucking sense.'

'But there's also this other type of song he does really well, where the writer is almost singing right into the listener's ear, and you know exactly where it's going, but you want to go anyway. I'm attracted to that angry Lennon, although it's another thing I haven't figured out how to do yet! He definitely deserves all the praise and accolades that he receives.'(lxxvi)

With the Olympics show a success, and eager to build on the momentum that R U Mine? had started, Arctic Monkeys decamped for sessions for their fifth album, first at Rancho De La Luna, Joshua Tree, with Josh Homme, before they took out a long lease on Sage & Sound Studios in LA, which became their de facto HQ for a period. The only updates fans received were from, wonderfully, Matt Helders' mother, who clarified some speculation on Twitter: 'I don't know if it helps to clear things up but lads are in the desert!' she wrote in September.

In March 2013, her son confirmed the album was coming at the *NME* Awards, at which the band picked up the Best Video Award for R U Mine?. 'I have been in the desert...with motorcycles. Not with Josh (Homme), no. The band's just been working together, the band working on our own so far, writing and stuff. There's no time deadlines or anything like that for release. We're just getting back into it because it always takes a while to get back into it.'

When asked what the album would sound

like, Helders replied, '2013'. The follow-up question as to if it would be released that calendar year was met with a deserved response: 'Well, we'd be stupid if we made a 2013 album and released it next year.'(lxxvii) Shortly afterward, Arctic Monkeys were confirmed as Friday headliners for Glastonbury Festival later that year.

The period in which the band recorded the new album was the first time since they were based in Sheffield that the four members of the group lived within the same area, which led to a more collaborative effort, all agreeing to borrow the architecture from their long-standing love of hip-hop but sustain a foundation of rock and roll.

R U Mine? was the blueprint and had inspired them to such a degree they were said to be fizzing with ideas for songs, but it wasn't until they had written one specific song that they had a definite answer as to which direction they would pursue. The track in question made its live debut during their comeback shows in the US and was selected as the next single, released shortly after Glastonbury Festival.

CHAPTER TEN
'Mad Sounds in Your Ears Make You Get Up and Dance' (2013)

Single 16:

Do I Wanna Know?
Released: 19th June 2013; UK Chart Position: 11;
Label: Domino; Album: *AM*
B-Side: 2013
Producers: James Ford and Ross Orton
All lyrics by Alex Turner; all music by Arctic Monkeys

While similar in aesthetic and lyrical content to R U Mine? with a parallel riff, Do I Wanna Know? stomps dustily rather than batters and is, atypically, quite conservative, and traditional in arrangement. There's little ambiguity as to what it's about; a lusty, near-infatuated set of lyrics, albeit still with some textbook Turner analogies ('Do you ever get that fear that you can't shift that sticks around like summat in your teeth?') but with an overt sexiness and yearning vocals. The bass throbs as the groove claps, the backing vocals and harmonies working in conjunction with the main vocal, Nick O'Malley supplying the low notes with Matt Helders on the highs before they all converge at the end.

The video was a first for the group; a full animation piece directed by David Wilson, it begins with simple visuals of sound waves (in the same style as the *AM* cover art) that vibrate in synchronisation with the instruments and vocals, until the chorus kicks in and the animation becomes focussed on road racing and female images, with flashes of full colour animation. Recalling the surrealistic style of Robert Crumb and possibly referencing the Gary Gutierrez animations from *The Grateful Dead Movie*, the video has been viewed over 1 billion times on *YouTube,* one of only 12 rock songs to achieve such a feat.

B-side 2013 has a similar groove and riff but increases in pace as it develops, as Turner both observes and bemoans the pace of technology in society, the Big Brother culture and omnipresence of Apple products weighing heavily on his mind ('On the back of a transmitter there's a little shiny fruit and it's coming after you,'). The single fell just short of the top 10, but its number 11 spot was still their highest charting since Fluorescent Adolescent.

<u>UK Singles Chart – Top 10 – 23rd June 2013:</u>

1. Blurred Lines – Robin Thicke/TI/Pharrell
2. The Other Side – Jason Derulo
3. La La La – Naughty Boy ft Sam Smith
4. Let Her Go – Passenger
5. Goin' Crazy – Dizzee Rascal/Robbie Williams
6. Get Lucky – Daft Punk ft Pharrell Williams
7. Dear Darlin' – Olly Murs
8. Wild – Jessie J/Big Sean/Dizzee Rascal
9. Everything Has Changed – Taylor Swift ft Ed Sheeran
10. Another Love – Tom Odell

....

11. Do I Wanna Know? – Arctic Monkeys

In conjunction with the single, the band announced their fifth album (*AM*), followed by the small matter of their Glastonbury headline slot. Speaking to Zane Lowe on Radio 1, Matt Helders was confident that the preparations were going well: 'I'm prepared for what it entails in a way, but I think in terms of preparation we can mould a different kind of setlist for it and have a bit more fun with it…so far I'm probably quietly confident, but I know as soon as I'm walking up the steps I'll be in a different place completely, I'll just be talking nonsense, walking around a lot.'(lxxviii)

Also speaking to Lowe, Alex Turner recalled their 2007 appearance: 'It's kind of like an otherworldly quality that Glastonbury Festival has, that can't be explained to someone that hasn't experienced the thing. At that time when we last played it, I'd never been there before, I didn't really know what it was, you know, and now I think I've been like every year it's been on since then, and somehow, I feel that makes me better equipped to play it this time, and all others really.'

'Glastonbury is like this old wise wizard or something, it kind of controls the tides of the rock 'n roll universe, and I perhaps understand that a little better this time. I've got a respect for it, you know. Maybe that wise wizard's got a respect for us now, don't know. Hopefully he'll turn the speakers on or whatever, turn us up a bit this time.'(lxxix)

After a brief cameo during Miles Kane's set earlier in the day, performing Standing Next to Me (and taking a photograph with Everton footballer Leighton Baines after the show), Alex Turner and his friends took to the Pyramid Stage as the sun set. The back of the famous stage was emblazoned with the group's initials (and the title of the new album) in LED lights while the bass drum on Matt Helders' kit (who marked the occasion by wearing leather chapped trousers and band T-shirt emblazoned with the logo of Brighton duo Royal Blood) had the Sheffield telephone area code 0114 written in masking tape. Nick O'Malley wore a leather jacket, Jamie Cook donned a full suit with a tie while Alex Turner was in a sparkly grey suit jacket, with touring keys player Tom Rowley making his first UK appearance.

The set was rapturously received from start to finish. A direct but varied rock 'n' roll show made up the main set before a string quartet joined the group for acoustic versions of Cornerstone and, as a special Glastonbury treat, Mardy Bum, with arrangements provided by Guy Garvey of Elbow. With UK debuts for R U Mine? and Mad Sounds, it was a triumphant performance capped off with a crowd singalong of Happy Birthday to Turner's mum Penny, watching from the side of the stage.

The setlist was:

Do I Wanna Know?
Brianstorm
Dancing Shoes
Don't Sit Down 'Cause I've Moved Your Chair
Teddy Picker
Crying Lightning
Brick By Brick
Fake Tales Of San Francisco
She's Thunderstorms
Old Yellow Bricks
Pretty Visitors
I Bet You Look Good on The Dancefloor
Do Me A Favour
R U Mine?
Mad Sounds

Fluorescent Adolescent
A Certain Romance
Cornerstone
Mardy Bum
When The Sun Goes Down
505

Speaking to the *NME* shortly after they came offstage, the band was elated, Turner declaring: 'I couldn't have asked for anything more really – it was cool, wasn't it? My favourite bit was the encore. But then again, the start, Do I Wanna Know? was absolutely amazing too. To see everybody moving like that blew me away.' Jamie Cook was equally moved, in his understated way: 'We couldn't have given it any more...I just enjoyed it all, beginning to end.'(lxxx)

Turner added: 'It's one of the best gigs we've ever done. Ever! Just because it's Glastonbury. It wasn't raining and...it's Glastonbury! This is the best it gets! You only ever do, like, five gigs like this. And that one was the one. You do big shows, big festivals all the time. But it's a different beast, Glastonbury. We'll carry on playing to a lot of people all over the summer, but it won't have that feeling we had just then. That feeling I can't describe. It felt like I was in outer space.' Nick O'Malley was more sanguine than his bandmates: 'I was saying to them in the encore that it felt like I was floating when I was up there, like I had rollerblades on or something! Honestly, I thought I'd be shitting it, but I just felt really calm, strangely calm!'(lxxxi)

The set wasn't entirely without criticism, however. Viewers watching on the BBC, who perhaps hadn't seen Arctic Monkeys for a few years, were bemused by Turner's accent and onstage theatrics (or 'showmanship shit', as he referred to it on stage) and were quick to take to social media. Bewildered, Turner responded: 'I've been pointing my hands for ages though! Maybe it's just the quiff confusing people? Jo Whiley just said I was channelling my inner Elvis, but I dunno man. It's not intentional!'(lxxxii)

Having already heard *AM* and deciding it was going to be an important record, the *NME* was given unprecedented access to Arctic Monkeys, allocating several covers to them over the summer and autumn of 2013. Speaking of the new album to the magazine, Turner described it as sounding 'like a Dr. Dre Beat, but we've given it an Ike Turner bowl-cut and sent it galloping across the desert of a Stratocaster.' When asked about the new sound and if it still sounded like the band playing in a room (as on *Suck It And See*), he responded: 'Essentially, that's what it is, but if you can find a way to manipulate the instruments or the sounds to the point where it sounds a bit like a hip-hop beat that'd be boss in your car, then I think there's something quite cool about that.'(lxxxiii)

As the summer wore on, with the group playing festivals and shows across Europe, they balanced live performances with promotion for the forthcoming album. Speaking of Josh Homme's contribution, Turner explained he was returning a favour having provided backing vocals on If I Had A Tail from Queens Of The Stone Age's 2013 album *...Like Clockwork:* 'The Josh thing was very much a case of one of us returning a back scratch to the other...he came down and sort of got us out of a little rut. It's just fun, it's friends, extended family now – (they) came round, had a fun night. His contribution to our record is really exciting, it's probably my favourite. The 30 seconds that he's in there is just, I dunno, it's like something that I've never heard before. Not to blow my own trumpet or anything, but you know what I'm saying.'(lxxxiv)

The Queens of The Stone Age singer returned the compliment, as he told the *NME:* 'I sang on the new Arctic Monkeys record. It's a really cool, sexy-after-midnight record. It's called *AM,* so I guess that's really obvious. And it's really good. It's really good. It's not disco, but it's like a modern, dancefloor sexy record. It's really good.'(lxxxv) With the hype machine in full flow, yet more fuel was added to the fire just before the album's release with another single.

Single 17:

Why'd You Only Call Me When You're High?
Released: 11th August 2013; UK Chart Position: 8;
Label: Domino; Album: *AM*
B-Side: Stop the World I Wanna Get Off with You
Producer: James Ford

Although Do I Wanna Know? was a good signifier, Why'd You Only Call Me When You're High? better represents its parent album. According to its creator, the song began life as a more traditional rock track before it went through several changes, eventually emerging as a fusion of Jurassic 5 and Timbaland, with a nod to Dr. Dre in the key sequence. More funk than rock, it slinks and slithers while the lyrics (concerning drunken text messages and booty calls past an appropriate time of night) scan beautifully, particularly on the bridge. The alteration on the final chorus, swapping 'call' to 'phone', is curious and unexplained. Its lyrical simplicity, along with the album, is one of the many reasons *AM* was so successful, as it spoke in a language that the audience could relate to.

The accompanying video, directed by Nabil Elderkin, featured Turner first in a bar with his bandmates (shot at the Howl at The Moon pub on Hoxton Street, in East London) before he staggers the streets (mainly the same Hoxton street on which the legendary video for The Verve's Bitter Sweet Symphony was filmed in 1997), hallucinating and seeing the recipient of the text messages he is sending. Eventually, he arrives at the wrong house, and Stephanie (the girl) sees 17 missed messages from 'Alex Band Guy' on her phone but opts to ignore them.

Further evidence of Turner's insatiable libido arrives on Stop the World I Wanna Get Off with You, a piano-driven, swaggering anecdote about a secret desire, possibly in a work environment (where the opportunities for temptation are heightened), with Turner urging a woman to take their chances while they can and succumb to their mutual lust. The track reached number 74 on the UK Singles Chart, while the A-side made the top 10, the first time Arctic Monkeys had done so in six years.

<u>UK Singles Chart – Top 10 – 18th August 2013:</u>

1. Burn – Ellie Goulding
2. Wake Me Up – Avicii
3. We Can't Stop – Miley Cyrus
4. Summertime Sadness – Lana Del Ray Vs Cedric Gervais
5. Applause – Lady Gaga
6. Trampoline – Tinie Tempah ft 2 Chainz
7. Blurred Lines – Robin Thicke/TI/Pharrell

8. **Why'd You Only Call Me When You're High? – Arctic Monkeys**
9. Holy Grail – Jay-Z ft Justin Timberlake
10. We Own the Night – Wanted

When *AM* was announced in June, several details were disclosed; as well as Homme's contribution, it was revealed that Bill Ryder-Jones (former guitarist with The Coral) would feature on one track. Most intriguing was that, for the first time, the lyrics of a song would be written by someone other than Turner (excluding a few fleeting contributions from other members of the group). They had adapted a poem by one of his heroes into a song, with I Wanna Be Yours originally a 1982 poem by John Cooper Clarke from his 1982 album *Zip Style Method.*

The legendary Mancunian poet was pleased to have been an inspiration. 'I think it's great the band have used it because I think it was always kind of a song. It's a poem that owes a great deal to popular music. I haven't heard their version yet, but I know it's gonna be great,' he told the *NME.*

'I think he's (Turner) a fantastic lyricist. He's always changing, and as a band they won't be pinned down. I like that album they made when they'd been to the States for the first time, they were so obviously Americanised. I think things like that are a strength, where you can make every new experience uniquely you. That's part of the secret of longevity.'(lxxxvi) With accordant patronage and promises of massive things, *AM* was finally released in September.

Album 5:

AM
Released: 9th September 2013; UK Chart Position: 1; Label: Domino
Track Listing: Do I Wanna Know?; R U Mine?; One For The Road; Arabella; I Want It All; No.1 Party Anthem; Mad Sounds; Fireside; Why'd You Only Call Me When You're High?; Snap Out Of It; Knee Socks; I Wanna Be Yours
Producers: James Ford and Ross Orton
All lyrics by Alex Turner; all music by Arctic Monkeys. R U Mine? written by Alex Turner and Nick O'Malley; Mad Sounds written by Alex Turner and Alan Smyth; I Wanna Be Yours written by Alex Turner and John Cooper Clarke

Another sonic departure for this ever-evolving band, *AM* is unquestionably influenced by R&B (a fact Turner and co freely admitted), both contemporary and classic. After the one-two slap of the first two singles, the initially slow groove of One for The Road hammers the point with another Dr. Dre-influenced beat. A flabby bass and chilling guitar from Cook add to the ghostly atmosphere, building as it reaches the middle eight before galloping to the final chorus. The subject is simply about outstaying one's welcome with a potential love interest, the once-prevalent poetry absent, making the line, 'all the cracks in blackout blinds cast patterns on the ceiling,' seem incongruous.

The analogies aren't gone for long though, returning accompanied by the rock. Although Arabella starts with a remarkably similar beat to the preceding track, the two main influences of the record coming together, the monster riff, 'inspired' by War Pigs by Black Sabbath, blows everything else in proximity away. It's as 'rawk' as they've ever been, and the title is Alex Turner's version of the siren from *Barbarella,* even referencing as much: 'She's got a Barbarella swimsuit and when she needs to shelter from reality, she takes a dip in my daydreams.'

Shamelessly and proudly evoking the debauchery of the 1970s, it's a bonanza of a song with a propulsive crescendo and strangled guitar, a product of Turner's plan to remove the fuzz from his pedal to achieve a clearer sound. Lastly, Arabella features another of the many running musical themes on the album: a call-and-response duel between lead and backing/harmony vocals.

The snarling, glam-rock I Want It All also features dual falsetto vocals with a tinny guitar wig-out beneath. Its snappiness is punctuated by a sequence of glorious shoo-wops which make up the mid-section and the lyric, 'leave me listening to the Stones, 2000 Light Years from Home,' was a literal line, Turner feeling no need to supply any additional subtext.

Though divided by turning the record (for purchasers of the vinyl), the following two tracks are similar and bring the pace down to a crawl. The jaded No. 1 Party Anthem plods grandiosely, a big, lighters-in-the-air ballad that Elton John would be proud to be associated with, complete with wobbly organ and piano played by James Ford. A sign of things to come, it documents a girl at a party who's 'having a sly indoor smoke, she calls the folks who run this her oldest friends.'

Mad Sounds apes solo John Lennon rather than Elton John but is equally indebted to the era, with a heavy West Coast influence that takes its time but is consciously basic in melody and musicianship. An ode to the power and beauty of music of all genres ('mad sounds in your ears make you get up and dance,'), it's credited to Turner and Alan Smyth from the early days of the group. According to Turner, the former producer had written a song with the same title (although not in the same style), and when strumming his guitar, the memory returned to the songwriter.

Along with Snap Out of It, Mad Sounds doesn't feature Matt Helders due to an injury the drummer had suffered (received when punching a wall while drunk). Eager not to lose momentum, the band drafted in Pete Thomas, most famous for being part of Elvis Costello & The Attractions, on interim percussion duties. The Matt Helders we are familiar with re-enters the fray with aplomb on Fireside, cajoling his bass drums like a rapidly bouncing basketball. The do-wops add to the shimmering quality as the rhythm section reflects the rolling, boiling pace, with added melancholic solo from Bill Ryder-Jones, rekindling his relationship with Turner from the *Submarine* sessions.

Snap Out of It gets the fingers clicking and the toes tapping, as the piano drives a straightforward pop song with added strut and vigour. The song was going nowhere until Thomas flew to LA and encouraged the band to persevere with it. One of their more inessential but maddeningly catchy singles.

The much-heralded contribution from Josh Homme arrives just in time for *AM*'s last hurrah, as he brings his swaggering and unmistakable croon to the breakdown in the middle of Knee Socks, offering a countermelody to complement the resolving riff. One of the album's more ambitious lyrics, it's hard to escape the impression that it's about Turner's former relationship with Alexa Chung, given that she was frequently photographed wearing knee socks. Despite the rattling music which nearly drowns it, the detailed melancholia prevails in lines such as, 'when I thought you might be mine in a small world on an exceptionally wet Tuesday night,' and 'when you walked around your house wearing my sky-blue Lacoste and your knee socks.'

Lastly, I Wanna Be Yours is the deep sigh after the painful memory. Initially a sharper-edged demo, on the suggestion of James Ford, it became a slow jam, with tremolo guitars and a drum machine. It swoops and sighs to create a mental image of sweat dripping from the walls of a cave and finds Alex Turner coming full circle with his infatuation with John Cooper Clarke, acknowledging that 'secrets I have held in my heart are harder to hide than I thought,' is a better line to accurately describe his feelings than he could ever compose.

Turner claimed his approach to writing was different, adding lyrics and melodies to basslines while also being inspired for lyrics through singing with a space echo on his microphone. Thematically, *AM* is about insecurity and doubt (hence the considerable number of question marks), with several verses structured as conversations. More obviously, the title has a dual function, being both a useful acronym for Arctic Monkeys, reflecting their state of mind at the time (as bands so often declare when they release a self-titled album) as well as telling tales of the wee small hours. Like *Whatever People Say I Am, That's What I'm Not,* it conjures up mental images of nightclubs, darkness, and mischief.

'I actually stole it from the Velvet Underground. I'll just confess that now and get it out of the way. The *VU* record, obviously,' Turner confirmed to Zane Lowe on his Radio 1 show. 'Summat about it feels like this record is exactly where we should be right now. So it felt right to just initial it.'(lxxxvii)

The album artwork was understated, featuring the waveforms on the cover image, with an inner picture of the foursome dressed in shirts and ties reminiscent of Kraftwerk. The increased use of piano pointed to the future, but the rest of the album felt achingly contemporary back in 2013 and it elevated them to unprecedented heights. Arctic Monkeys were no longer just the preserve of indie and rock fans; hipsters and misfits alike loved *AM* and it brought them crashing into the centre of the mainstream once again, more forcefully than before.

It was no surprise that the *NME,* long since flag-wavers for the group, were impressed but they surpassed themselves in their praise. In a five-star review, Mike Williams declared 'it might be *the* greatest record of the last decade...a band who will not look back on this record as a career-high, but as the moment they stopped being defined by genre and instead became artists. Not a rock band, definitely not an indie band, but artists. Think Bowie, think The Beatles, think Stevie Wonder and think Bob Dylan.'(lxxxviii)

But they weren't alone in their praise. *The Guardian* called it 'their most coherent, most satisfying album since their debut'(lxxxix) while *Time Out* was confident that 'one of Britain's greatest bands just got greater in an unexpected but hugely welcome way.'(xc) *Q* Magazine gave it a 4/5 review, as Matt Mason wrote: 'Not afraid to explore but never radical for the sake of it, Arctic Monkeys have delivered another triumph…not for the first time, they sound like the best band in Britain.' Even *Pitchfork* was impressed, giving *AM* 8 marks out of 10. Two days after its release, AM was nominated for the Mercury Music Award, itself a remarkable feat.

Predictably, *AM* went straight in at number 1 on the UK Album Chart with first-week sales of 157,329 copies, making it the second-fastest-selling album of 2013 (after Daft Punk's much-anticipated *Random Access Memories*). Both records, along with David Bowie's comeback album *The Next Day,* helped boost vinyl sales hit a ten-year peak in 2013. It also made the top 10 in the US, selling 42,000 copies to get a number 6 placing on the *Billboard* chart, just falling short of *Favourite Worst Nightmare's* sales figures, also setting a record as the first act on an independent label to achieve five consecutive number ones.

UK Album Chart – Top 10 – 15th September 2013:

1. ***AM* – Arctic Monkeys**
2. *If You Wait* – London Grammar
3. *The 1975* – The 1975
4. *Tales Of Us* – Goldfrapp
5. *Snapshot* – The Strypes
6. *Time* – Rod Stewart
7. *The Impossible Dream* – Richard & Adam
8. *All The Little Lights* – Passenger
9. *Bad Blood* – Bastille
10. *Long Way Down* – Tom Odell

During the promotion of the album, the group cited their influences during recording. Jamie Cook revealed that David Bowie's seminal 1972 album *The Rise and Fall of Ziggy Stardust and The Spiders From Mars* was on heavy rotation during the sessions, while Alex Turner was quick to praise rapper Drake as an influence and, accordingly, the group performed his hit Hold On, We're Going Home for their semi-regular appearance on the *Live Lounge.*

When discussing their new-found (relative) eagerness to engage with the media, Nick O'Malley proffered an obvious explanation for their previous reluctance. 'In the early days, when we were getting asked questions, we were 18 or 19 and you don't even talk that much to your friends. With lads, it's, 'All right?' 'Yeah.' There's lots of very basic grunting,' he told *The Observer.* 'Now, once you get older, it gets a little bit easier. We've all developed our conversational skills.'(xci)

In a sign of things to come, Alex Turner told the *NME* in September: 'I'm not really that up for playing guitar at the moment, so I'm trying to get everybody else to do it.' In the same feature, Jamie Cook commented on the band's ever-increasing international touring: 'That's the thing. We love touring. We just love playing shows. It's like, we can do the UK, but it's a small place – three weeks and you're done. And then how many shows can you do on an album. We aren't (keen on) shoving it down people's throats.'

Meanwhile, in a statement that would confirm the mentality of the group and their continued attempts to break the United States, Alex Turner disclosed: 'I definitely have ambitions to keep progressing in America, because it's come so far in the past few years. You can just tell. I think you see something starting to happen over there. It's hard to leave that alone.'(xcii)

CHAPTER ELEVEN
'Secrets I Have Held In My Heart Are Harder To Hide Than I Thought' (2013-2017)

The latest leg of an extensive North American tour spanned a month between mid-September and mid-October 2013 before some arena shows in the UK: Newcastle, Manchester, London, Liverpool (where they covered Walk on The Wild Side as a tribute to the recently deceased Lou Reed) and Cardiff as well as European dates.

Arctic Monkeys were forced to postpone three further UK shows as Alex Turner contracted laryngitis. After a rescheduled homecoming gig at the Motorpoint Arena, they played Birmingham and Glasgow before heading back to the US in late November. In amongst all the touring they announced two huge outdoor shows at Finsbury Park in London, scheduled for May of the following year, with support coming from Miles Kane and Royal Blood, a new favourite of the band.

So galvanised were they by the recording and positive response to *AM,* there was talk of a 'sequel,' which Turner refused to rule out: 'I think I can see there being something...I can't really confirm or deny that one. I can sort of imagine what it might be. I could see it when the record was finished. We'd met the deadline, but the thing was still sort of snowballing a little bit, and for that reason, we could still find ourselves walking into another one...the songs aren't there, it's just an idea of mine. But that's usually how it works: this time the idea definitely led the whole procession, rather than the songs themselves.'(xciii)

The spooky One for The Road was released as the fourth single in December 2013, endorsed with a gloomy video (directed by Focus Creeps) suitable for the season, shot in black-and-white with Cook taking the limelight as the main protagonist for once, driving a tractor through cornfields in Mendota, Illinois while his band mates struck poses and played their instruments against a backdrop of fireworks and models.

On B-Side You're So Dark, Turner sings in a disaffected voice about a goth girl who has her 'unkind of ravens and murder of crows,' and is also a fan of H.P. Lovecraft and Italian horror, organs adding to the Transylvanian vibes. However, the single couldn't capitalise on the success of Why'd You Only Call Me When You're High? and peaked at a lowly 114.

Single 18:

One For the Road
Released: 9th December 2013; UK Chart Position: N/A; Label: Domino; Album: *AM*
B-Side: You're So Dark
Producers: James Ford and Ross Orton

The *AM* tour recommenced at the end of January in Miami, the challenging work of charming the United States starting to reap dividends. Although a new measurement, Arctic Monkeys were revealed to have more mentions on the microblogging site Tumblr than Lady Gaga, at that point the biggest pop star in the world.

Meanwhile, to commemorate 50 years since

The Beatles' legendary appearance on *The Ed Sullivan Show* (watched by a reported 73 million viewers), they performed a cover of All My Loving during a headline show at Madison Square Garden in New York. It was also announced in February that the group would headline both T In the Park in Scotland and Reading & Leeds Festivals for the second time as well as, more significantly, Lollapalooza in Chicago.

By now one of the biggest bands in the world, the music press understandably felt the need to ask the group for their insights on the state of the industry, and Matt Helders duly obliged to the *NME*: 'Maybe guitar bands will come back around again and reclaim the charts, but it's all very well me saying that – it all comes down to them: they've got to have the songs that are good enough to play on the radio. But if guitars are a dirty word at the moment, then I like that, I think that's a good thing. When it's popular, it feels like there's something weird going on – like you've hijacked the charts. That's how we felt when it happened to us, even though there were still a lot of guitar bands around at the time. We didn't even expect our first single to get into the Top 20, so we definitely felt like we shouldn't have been there.'(xciv)

Awards season found the Arctic Monkeys as the name on everybody's lips after a few years' absence, with two nominations at the Brit Awards: Best Album and Best British Group. The group opened the event at London's o2 Arena in style, playing R U Mine?, a track that had now usurped I Bet You Look Good on The Dancefloor as their calling card, while the two letters of their recent album were set ablaze in the middle of the arena (at the behest of the event organisers).

The quartet, specifically Alex Turner, were in vainglorious mood. After winning Best British Group and taking to the stage, the singer turned to Matt Helders and said, 'Well there's that £15 we put on One Direction to win it down t'drain innit?' Referring to some of the lengthy acceptance speeches that had already taken place, he continued: 'there's a lot of people that require thanks for this, but they need to hear their names read out about as much as you need to hear another list of people you don't know, so thank you for the acknowledgment and have a wonderful evening,' before carefully placing the microphone on to the podium.

But it was their second acceptance speech that made the headlines. After taking to the podium to accept Best Album, as his bandmates looked on and whispered amongst themselves (with Cook looking slightly unimpressed, it must be said), Turner took the opportunity to deliver a monologue.

'That rock 'n' roll, eh? That rock 'n' roll, it just won't go away. It might hibernate from time to time, sink back into the swamp. I think the cyclical nature of the universe in which it exists demands it adheres to some of its rules. But it's always waiting there just around the corner. Ready to make its way back through the sludge and smash through the glass ceiling, looking better than ever.'

'Yeah, that rock 'n' roll, it seems like it's faded away sometimes, but it will never die. And there's nothing you can do about it. Thank you very much for this, I do truly appreciate it. Don't take that the wrong way. And yeah...invoice me for the microphone if you need to.' He then proceeded to stretch his arm out and drop the mic, which unfortunately didn't make the feedback noise that was presumably intended.

It was an odd speech but in keeping with Turner's previous comments about the responsibility that lay upon his band's shoulders, while also a rallying cry for the genre his band best represented. However, it was undermined by his stopping himself from saying, 'thank you very fucking much,' which would have underlined his point better. In the post-ceremony interviews, Nick O'Malley made his bandmate's point more succinctly: 'He just basically meant, rock 'n' roll will never die and there's nothing you can do about it. That's the gist.'

When asked if awards were important to him, Turner was appreciative but resolute: 'I refuse to put too much importance on these things. I've got a lot of respect for these ceremonies, but it's not what we do it for and it never was. A band or a group or an artist's talent is not directly proportional to the size of their trophy cabinet. It's the opposite of Moto Grand Prix, when that is very much the case.'(xcv)

The speech quickly became infamous and got a very mixed response on social media, yet along with David Bowie's speech (delivered by Kate Moss) requesting Scotland vote 'No' in the forthcoming independence referendum, it lit up an otherwise anodyne evening. It followed Turner around for months and he was forced to explain himself on countless occasions. 'I'm in a difficult position in the sense that, preposterous as it might sound, I don't like being the centre of attention. I get up onstage every night and play songs, but I almost feel the songs are the centre of attention. I don't like opening my birthday presents in front of people, either. But I can't really see another way round making an acceptance speech,' he explained.

'I suppose on some level, in that environment, rightly or wrongly, it almost feels like we were representatives of guitar music, or rock'n'roll. And while I don't see getting any trophy as a great victory, in some sense it's a victory for our music. But I can't go up and gush about how I dreamt about picking up a Brit Award all my life, because it just isn't the truth.'(xcvi)

Turner elaborated further at the *NME* Awards the following week: 'It's not aggressive. It's just about presenting an option that people may or may not know exists. It occurred to me that in that room, or certainly watching it on TV, were people who'd never heard the term 'rock 'n' roll' other than to describe a zip on a Topman jacket.'

'I don't see it as a personal victory, but it seems in some way a victory for bands and the idea that you can start a band with your mates and eventually go on to move people, or whatever you wanna call it. Using rock'n'roll as the most direct way of illustrating that was kinda what I was trying to do.'(xcvii) There was less controversy at the more comfortable environs of the *NME* Awards, Turner and Helders keeping their speeches to a minimum and simply thanking the voters, although the former did acknowledge that he'd 'used all my best shit last week', as they picked up five gongs included Best Album, Best Band and Best Live Band.

Arabella was selected as the fifth single to be lifted from *AM* but, although given heavy airplay in the early part of 2014, a physical release of the single was cancelled, and no B-side was released. However, the cancellation took place after the video was unveiled, another black-and-white piece featuring the group performing the song in a small bikers' club.

Single 19:

Arabella
Released: 10th March 2014 (radio); UK Chart Position: 155; Label: Domino; Album: *AM*

Producers: James Ford and Ross Orton

After a three-month break, the *AM* tour recommenced in Australia and, while down under they performed a cover of Feels Like We Only Go Backwards by Tame Impala, recently announced as support for the forthcoming Finsbury Park shows. In the lead-up to the mega-gigs, Alex Turner revealed how comfortable the group felt playing to larger audiences: 'Playing large shows has, to some degree, become second nature. We've been around the block a few times now,' he told *NME.* 'I saw the Stones at Glastonbury and they've been doing it since they were a lot younger than I am now, and it still seemed like it meant a lot to them. Honestly, the reason we're most excited about it is that we don't get to play the UK as much as we used to, just because of the way it is now. Any chance to come home – or as close to home as London – is exciting for us.'

In the same interview, Matt Helders expressed doubt that there would be much older material at the shows: 'We kind of felt that way about Glastonbury, that we should play songs like Mardy Bum or Fake Tales Of San Francisco but it didn't really get the response I thought it would. I know people will still have a massive affiliation with that first album in England, but I think they've also moved on from it a bit as well.'(xcviii) As it transpired, Alex Turner did perform an acoustic version of A Certain Romance for the 45,000 people in attendance at the north London shows on the first night, with Miles Kane joining Turner onstage for an acoustic version of The Last Shadow Puppets' Standing Next To Me the following day.

The setlists were:

Do I Wanna Know?
Snap Out of It
Arabella
Brianstorm
Don't Sit Down 'Cause I've Moved Your Chair
Dancing Shoes
Library Pictures
Crying Lightning
Why'd You Only Call Me When You're High/I Bet You Look Good on The Dancefloor
Fireside/She's Thunderstorms
I Bet You Look Good on The Dancefloor/No.1 Party Anthem
She's Thunderstorms/Why'd You Only Call Me When You're High?
No.1 Party Anthem/Fireside
Cornerstone
Knee Socks
Fluorescent Adolescent
505
A Certain Romance/Standing Next to Me
One For the Road
I Wanna Be Yours
R U Mine?

To accompany the shows, an unprecedented sixth single was lifted from *AM*, with Snap Out of It hitting number 84 in the UK charts, the second in succession to be released without a B-side. The Focus Creeps-directed video featured actor Stephanie Sigman as an obsessed Arctic Monkeys fan watching home videos of the group in the studio while cavorting around her apartment.

Single 20:

Snap Out of It
Released: 9th June 2014; UK Chart Position: 82;
Label: Domino; Album: *AM*
Producers: James Ford and Ross Orton

After Finsbury Park, Alex Turner revealed that, for once, he felt no urgent need to craft the follow-up to *AM,* as the group's success in America was still to be exploited. 'I've written a few things, but I'm not in a hurry,' he told the *NME.* 'We're going to keep going until the summer and beyond that a little bit, maybe. I don't know. I wouldn't think it'll be too soon that we do the next one…it's been going really well in America and there's still lots of shit still to do on this album. I don't feel, for once, that we need to rush and get on to the next thing. It seems like a good place to leave it for a minute.'(xcix)

Meanwhile, his fellow Last Shadow Puppet revealed that the pair were writing a screenplay before they opted to make music together again. When asked about new music, Miles Kane told *NME:* 'It's something we always talk about, y'know? But I think we're gonna write this film first anyway before we hit back into that…it's gonna have a sort of *X-Men* kind of vibe and sort of set in the '60s, but I can't give any more away than that.'(c) Elsewhere, it was revealed in *The Times* newspaper that Arctic Monkeys were reported to have each paid between £38,000 and £84,000 in fees to an organisation called Liberty to apparently protect their earnings between 2005 and 2009.

Yet another busy summer concluded with a headline set at Reading & Leeds Festivals after a well-received set at T In the Park. In the lead-up, Matt Helders commented that the group felt more comfortable as headliners: 'We've got better, now we're more ready to headline festivals. Before, it was more because of demand. Still, we held off from a lot of things pretty well in terms of doing stuff like arena tours. We did the second-to-last slot (in 2006) then the headline; it felt like we built up to it. But as a band and as performers, if I dare say that, I feel we've got better at it.' Asked about the big shows, he acknowledged, 'Everything changes. All of a sudden there's loads more people there working for you. I like it, it gets exciting. It feels like something big's happening.'(ci)

Elsewhere, Turner confirmed the sets would be the last chance UK audiences would have to see the foursome for some time: 'We've seen a lot of festival crowds over the last 10 summers but this one (Leeds) is different, especially for us as it's the one we were once a part of. Like when we were youths, it's a weekend we are once again very much looking forward to and it seems like the perfect place to leave things for a while.'(cii) As they were back on home turf, Turner wore a white rose in each lapel (the symbol of Yorkshire) and changed the words on Old Yellow Bricks to include the line, 'Oh Sheffield is wonderful.'

The fireworks at the end of the show fading into the sky signified the last time Arctic Monkeys would be seen in the UK for four years, although they did perform another 10 shows in North America and 6 in South America towards the end of 2014. After nearly 10 years at the top and on the back of their biggest album, Arctic Monkeys finally took some well-earned time off.

Not that the members were inactive for the

next few years. In March 2015, Alex Turner popped up on the track Vertigo by Mini Mansions. The American group consisted of Queens of The Stone Age bassist Michael Shurman, Tyler Parkford, and Zach Dawes (who would later go on to collaborate with The Last Shadow Puppets). Turner delivered the second verse on Vertigo and appeared in the video for the single, as well as appearing onstage with the group on a handful of occasions. The frontman was also listed as co-writer for the track Risk (Demo) by Portland-based singer/songwriter Alexandra Savior, the song appearing on the soundtrack for the popular HBO series *True Detective.*

The following month, *AM* was announced as the top-selling vinyl album of the decade so far, followed by Radiohead's *The King of Limbs, Random Access Memories* by Daft Punk, and a brace of Pink Floyd albums: *Dark Side Of The Moon* and *The Endless River.* Even more impressively, Arctic Monkeys were listed as the second most-streamed artist on Spotify in 2014 (after Ed Sheeran), and *AM* was crowned as the *NME*'s best album of the decade at the halfway mark. Meanwhile, the forgotten man of the band, Andy Nicholson, set up a new record label in 2015, Card Gang Music, promising a home to eclectic offerings, and the former bassist revealed that he was close friends with his former band and the door to his Sheffield studio was always open.

While 2015 was the quietest year to date for the group, it soon became apparent how two of its members had been occupying their time. Shortly after the death of his close friend David Bowie, music legend Iggy Pop announced a new album in January 2016, recorded in secret with a new band consisting of Josh Homme, fellow Queen of The Stone Age Dean Fertita, with one Matt Helders on drums. Homme revealed that, after initial meetings with Pop, it was decided that a temporary band was required, and he coerced Helders into playing drums for the album and preceding tour.

Recorded in early 2015 at Homme's Rancho De La Luna studio (by now a familiar haunt for Helders), *Post Pop Depression* was released in March 2016 and became Iggy Pop's most successful album to date, hitting the top 20 in the US and top 5 in the UK. Ensuring that the aura of the project was maintained, the supergroup played only a handful of dates in the spring of 2016, with the shows allowing Helders to drum on some classic rock songs, including The Passenger, China Girl, Sister Midnight as well as the iconic Lust for Life. Their show at the Royal Albert Hall in London was released as a live album towards the end of 2016, while Helders also played drums on the opening track from Lady Gaga's album *Joanne* (Diamond Heart).

In December 2015, The Last Shadow Puppets' social media accounts released two short videos announcing their return in Spring 2016, while on 10th January (a few days after Alex Turner's 30th birthday), they released the first single from their second album: a lurking, squealing, Miles Kane-sung track called Bad Habits. The song had emerged from a jam session that had lasted 40 minutes while the video featured a performance of the song in a tiny club environment.

It was announced that their second album had been recorded in the summer of 2015 at producer Rick Rubin's Shangri-La studios in Malibu, California and the act was expanded to incorporate Zach Dawes from Mini Mansions as well as James Ford, Turner, and Kane. The album was christened *Everything You've Come to Expect,* to be released on

1st April and would feature a cover image of Tina Turner.

In a launch interview in the *NME,* Turner explained the influences on the album: 'I think that last record ended up being just one thing. We talked about Scott Walker a lot and our record became perceived as a homage to that sound. This one, in my head, doesn't wear its influences on its sleeve as much as the first one did. We were definitely listening to a bit of Isaac Hayes this time, but it was less of a big deal.'(ciii)

In the same feature, Turner referenced their latest look. Gone were the smart suits, Chelsea boots, and mop-top haircuts, to be replaced with more striking colours and casual outfits. Turner's accurate description of the new attire? 'We've gone from The Beatles to *The Fast and The Furious.*'

Elsewhere in the wide-ranging interview, Turner revealed the broader plans for the project: 'Well, we wanted it to be a trilogy. We wanted to write the second and third parts before we released the second.' When asked if the third album was imminent Turner replied hesitantly: 'Well, I don't know about that. There are lots of other things we have to factor in.'

String arranger Owen Pallett also offered a behind-the-curtain perspective into the different approaches of the two songwriters: 'Miles always had knee-jerk reactions to the music where he'd go, 'No, it's supposed to go like this!' Alex is more of a slow burner. Sometime around 2am, after we'd had a few drinks, he'd go, 'That part of the song isn't working. We should do it this way.' I'd make a note and fix it in the morning.'(civ)

The promotional activity portrayed Kane and Turner as lotharios living the high life in California and indeed the album was certainly less serious than *The Age of The Understatement,* being almost silly at points. However, Kane ran into trouble, later apologising for an 'ill-judged sexual remark' as well as a 'not-entirely consensual kiss on the cheek' involving *Spin* journalist Rachel Brodsky during an interview in New York.

Everything You've Come to Expect has a clearer divide between the songs written by Turner and Kane, if we can assume that the lead singer of the track is the main architect (although all bar three are credited as joint compositions). The stalking, menacing Used to Be My Girl is the only song to feature joint singing, with the rest divided between the two with the other as support.

The strongest tie to the first album, Miracle Aligner contains Scott Walker-esque strings, notable for being co-written by Turner and Alexandra Savior, and was presumably a product of their writing sessions. Turner sings the lilting melody alone which, yet again, covers carnal matters: 'He was born to blow your mind or something along those lines tonight.'

A sexual encounter in a wooded glade is the subject matter of the dark, so-so She Does the Woods while on Sweet Dreams, TN Turner yearns and strains his voice while not hiding behind metaphors or analogies ('Could I have made it any clearer?') to air his hurt and regret over lost love. For that reason alone, it's unique in Turner's canon, with no understatement or subtlety.

The remaining solo Turner composition (The Dream Synopsis), picks up where Mad Sounds left off; a slow, Leonard Cohen-indebted track with Turner facing the realisation that his insecurities have ruined past relationships: 'visions of the past and possible future shoot through my mind and I can't let go.' He goes one step further on bonus track The Bourne Identity as he admits, 'I'm done beating myself up, there'll be nothing left to love.'

Turner is supported by Kane on vocals on the flabby Dracula Teeth, with the latter delivering his trademark guitar tones, while the Blaxploitation influence is most keenly felt on the jerky The Element of Surprise, with Matt Helders providing backing vocals, as he does on Used To Be My Girl and the title track. Kane takes lead vocals on the luscious single Aviation, originally intended for a solo album of his own, and the forgettable Pattern.

The album's centrepiece (and the song the group was most proud of) is the title track, all falsetto vocals, and a dreamy but simple melody. The lyrics verge on nonsensical and are littered with references to other songs, artists, and albums: Diamond Dog (David Bowie), Honey Pie (The Beatles), Four Horsemen (American band), Shadowplay (Joy Division), and Holy Bible (Manic Street Preachers). Included among the references are other unusual phrases: 'tiger eyelashes', 'dirtbag ballet', and the 'chalet of the shadow of death.'

The album has its moments, but its unashamedly sleazy nature does get wearing, although it is musically accomplished and improves over time. The reception was positive, hitting number 1 in the UK, with several UK gigs at mid-sized venues across the spring and summer of 2016.

During the promotional trail for *Everything You've Come to Expect,* Alex Turner revealed in an interview on BBC Radio 4's *Front Row* that the lyrics were consciously different from those he would usually use in Arctic Monkeys' songs: 'Going into this second album I remembered the Puppets was a vehicle for me to try new things for the first time. Before that record, every song I'd ever written was based on a very real scenario. The first Shadow Puppets record was the first time I attempted to step away from that. Most of the time it came out pretty silly. But there were a few moments where it worked out.'

Turner also revealed that his approach to singing was different, with only The Dream Synopsis finding him delivering in his usual manner: 'I don't remember ever thinking about my voice before (*The Age of The Understatement*). The idea of singing never occurred to me then. I'd just write these things, and my voice was a vehicle for getting the words out. The melody isn't something I'd considered, but it's as powerful as the melodic aspect of the song, if not more so.'

'There's a line in the chorus (of The Dream Synopsis) where I say it must be awful to hear me talk about my dreams. In a way I'm talking to people who were fans of the very immediate, observational lyrics I wrote at the beginning.' (cv)

The Last Shadow Puppets lifted a further three singles from the second album: Everything You've Come to Expect, Aviation (which had linked videos, the latter being a prequel to the former), and Miracle Aligner. In addition, they performed on the Pyramid Stage at Glastonbury Festival, covering Moonage Daydream by David Bowie as a tribute to the icon, one of many acknowledgements at the festival. Elsewhere, at Manchester's Castlefield Bowl, the group was joined onstage for a cover of The Smiths' Last Night I Dreamt Somebody Loved Me by Johnny Marr, one of the song's original architects.

Another cover from their live sets (The Fall's Totally Wired), was included on an EP released at the end of 2016 to round off a busy year. Recorded in one day at Future-Past Studios, the songs featured were recorded live, with new versions of Aviation and The Dream Synopsis comprising the first and last tracks. In addition, the group covered This Is Your Life by Glaxo Babies, originally released in 1979, Jacques Dutronc's Les Cactus from 1967 (featuring Turner singing in French), and Is This What You Wanted, lifted from Leonard Cohen's fourth studio album *New Skin for The Old Ceremony*.

Meanwhile, rumours started circling that Arctic Monkeys had returned to the studio in 2016, denied by the band's spokesperson, who could do little to stop a photograph of the group leaking onto social media in 2016. Before that, it was revealed that Alex Turner had spent further time writing with American singer Alexandra Savior, co-writing, and producing (as well as playing bass, guitars, keyboards, and synthesizers on, along with James Ford and Zach Dawes) her debut album *Belladonna of Sadness,* released in April 2017.

All tracks on the album are listed as co-writes between Savior and Turner apart from Bones (listed as a Turner-only composition), while Ford is also listed on Audeline. While the songs on *Belladonna of Sadness* are structured more traditionally, with logical melodic sequencing, musically it's a precursor to the next Arctic Monkeys album. With her voice high in the mix, Savior immerses herself in the songs but the presence of Turner and, more pertinently, Ford, permeates the entire record.

Shimmering sci-fi keys and retro musicianship abound on the likes of Mirage and Shades, while Frankie has an immediately recognisable dull, dubby stomp. Indeed, the latter track best represents the transition from *AM* to

Tranquility Base Hotel + Casino; the pacing and chorus recall Knee Socks, but the instrumentation and sounds are more reminiscent of the sixth album.

Shades has echoing drums and dramatic, irregular guitar while the gentle tambourine rustle on Girlie punctuates a Portishead-esque sparseness and elegance. It's easy to imagine Turner on lead vocals, the sort of glacial melodrama that he excels at, along with his trademark Western guitar which peppers the album. Furthermore, certain lyrical vignettes scream as his creations, although it's not made clear as to who wrote what on the co-compositions. 'She's almost like a million other people that you'll never get to know and it feels as if she's swallowing me whole,' (Mirage) sounds very much like the sort of thought that would run through Turner's head, as does 'Strawberry split personality, she's got so many years hanging over me,' from 'Til You're Mine.

M.T.M.E has an economical chorus ('Scribble down in pencil, ten-track souvenir, audio memento, music to my ears,'), a trick that would often be utilised moving forward, but best of all is a lyric from Vanishing Point: 'Spectacular blacklight posting neon sky to which the sun so quickly unsubscribes,' is the sort of poetry and mixed metaphor that Turner relishes.

Likewise, the closing lines of Mystery Girl: 'I know that we're growing apart because you planted the seeds yourself.' The one solo composition (Bones) continues the insecure romantic questioning of *AM* ('Don't know how my head's in such a spin, is yours in one too, baby?') but is otherwise concise and features much lyrical repetition.

If it needs repeating, *Belladonna of Sadness* cements the realisation of how much of Alex Turner's creativity is steered by James Ford, which is not to undermine Savior's contribution, whose vocals humanise the album, but it does appear to be a construct from the two men. In an interview with *MusicFeeds,* the singer explained how the collaboration came about: 'It started out with me writing. I had just been signed to Columbia for about five months and I had been writing and I think that they wanted me to have some co-writers.'

'Alex, I had sent him some of my stuff, and we met up for coffee. It wasn't really planned that we would do the whole record together; I don't think anything was really expected. I didn't really think anything of it, but it ended up that after writing one song we just sort of decided to make the whole record and that's how James came in, he does all of Alex's records. James was really the genius behind the whole thing, getting that really lovely sound he's able to bring out.'(cxxv)

Although it received positive reviews, *Belladonna of Sadness* went unnoticed by the mainstream, its lack of impact creating the impression that the style of *Tranquility Base Hotel + Casino* came completely out of leftfield. When viewed in context it, alongside *Everything You've Come to Expect,* represents clear and logical steps on Turner and Ford's creative journey to the next Arctic Monkeys album.

CHAPTER TWELVE
'I Just Wanted to Be One of The Strokes. Now Look at The Mess You Made Me Make' (2017-2018)

Belladonna of Sadness aside, 2017 was a quiet year in the public eye for Arctic Monkeys as they hunkered down to record their sixth album. It was later revealed that, following the international success of *AM,* Alex Turner had been suffering from a form of writer's block, a fact he had alluded to in interviews but was masked by the band's excessive touring across 2013/14.

In early 2016, the frontman watched Federico Fellini's 1963 film *8 ½* and realised that he had been struggling to foster any new musical ideas. Having written Sweet Dreams, TN, his most honest love letter to date and a culmination of his period of writing love songs, he felt there were few other avenues he could explore within that one subject and, after watching Fellini's depiction of writer's block (along with accessing childhood memories and the science fiction genre), ironically found inspiration to compose.

However, Turner's muse was to be found not on guitar, but on the Steinway Vertegrand piano he had been gifted by Arctic Monkeys' manager Ian McAndrew for his 30th birthday. 'It was quite a rush, really,' Turner told *Billboard* in 2018. 'Prior to that point I didn't really have many ideas, and in my memory, that was the point at which they started to come. Sitting at the piano took me immediately to a different place. There are chords that came out, my fingers were falling (at) different places, and the sounds were giving me ideas. That I was the guy sitting at the piano also gave me ideas.'

'With the commercial success of the last record, I don't think I felt the pressure of that hanging over the creative process. But there was a pressure, in that we step it up and do something different again – try and fly high.'(cvi)

Turner began writing demos in the same style as the songs written with Alexandra Savior in a spare room of his Los Angeles home, re-christened Lunar Surface, while recalling the piano lessons he had received from his father when he was a boy. In addition, he took his approach from his hero Leonard Cohen, merging abstract lyrical ideas to make a coherent whole. Eventually, with enough tracks to begin working on, Jamie Cook was invited to hear the fruits of Turner's labour in early 2017. 'I was blown away by the direction Alex had gone in,' he revealed to *Rolling Stone,* 'It took a few listens to even begin to......it was just, like, 'Shit. What do we do with *this*?'(cvii).

The four members of the group converged at La Frette studios in Paris and Vox Studios in Hollywood, inviting a host of outside musicians to contribute. As well as James Ford, guitarist Tom Rowley (a touring member of the band since 2013) featured on several tracks, as did Zach Dawes and Tyler Parkford of Mini Mansions. Loren Humphrey of American rock band Guards, James Righton (formerly of nu-rave act Klaxons), pianist Josephine Stephenson and Evan Weiss from Wires on Fire also contributed instrumentation to the sixth album, while Cam Avery of Tame Impala provided backing vocals. Influenced by images of the sessions for the Beach Boys' masterpiece *Pet Sounds* and Dion's *Born to Be with You,* the musicians performed together in a single room to capture similar vibes.

The usual boundaries and constraints in which the band had worked seemed to be lifted; while Turner was primarily on piano, he would often be joined by Cook or would play drums alongside Matt Helders, with Ford also stepping in. Meanwhile, images of Nick O'Malley showed him playing the acoustic guitar as well as his traditional bass. Matt Helders would later comment that his minimal drumming was intended to serve the songs and indeed, while it may have appeared remiss to minimalize the greatest drummer of his generation's contribution, it must be said that the songs don't suit his normal breathless and spontaneous style.

Arctic Monkeys announced a series of international festival slots in early 2018, at the likes of Primavera and NOS Alive, along with a headline slot at the TRNSMT festival in Glasgow, further ramping the anticipation. Finally, on 5th April 2018, Arctic Monkeys released a short video trailer on their YouTube page, announcing their first album in nearly 5 years: *Tranquility Base Hotel + Casino*. The 42-second trailer featured the model that would adorn the artwork and was soundtracked by an alternative, keyboard version of Four Out of Five before the song's riff. The track list and artwork were also announced on the same date, alongside a host of summer dates around the world.

As the release date approached, snippets of information about this mysterious project were revealed. Speaking with *Mojo,* Jamie Cook revealed that there had been conversations about releasing *Tranquility Base Hotel + Casino* as a solo album for Turner: 'I think, at first, because it was quite basic – piano, vocal and no guitar – Al was in two minds about, 'is this Arctic Monkeys or am I going somewhere else with this'...and maybe at first I was a bit like that as well. It's definitely not a guitar-heavy record, not typically what we'd do. It took a lot more thinking about.'(cviii)

Meanwhile, the head of Sony, Arctic Monkeys' publishers, added to the speculation. When interviewed by *Music Week*, Guy Moot declared the album as Turner's best work: 'There are few releases in the calendar year that I would call an event; when the Monkeys release a record, it's an event. It's the sort of record people will stop their day to listen to it and rush to their streaming accounts or however they consume it. It's a big event for the UK music industry. It's an ongoing chapter and I think (Alex Turner's) just written another masterpiece, which solidifies him once more as one of the great UK songwriters.'(cix)

Unusually, it soon became apparent that there would be no lead single for the album, nor would any other song be unveiled before its release. While being a highly unusual tactic, it was the sort of thing a band of their status could execute in tandem with being an excellent marketing tool of its own, to sustain and build anticipation. From an artistic perspective, *Tranquility Base Hotel + Casino* works best consumed as one complete piece of work, so the decision made sense, even if it was frustrating for fans.

In the weeks leading up to release, Arctic Monkeys managed expectations by releasing a playlist of songs that had influenced the album, which included Nite Flights by The Walker Brothers, Baltimore by Nina Simone, Did She Mention My Name by Dr. John, Looking for You by Nino Ferrer and General Confessional by The Electric Prunes among its 26 tracks. Meanwhile, in an interview with *Intro,* Turner revealed that the possibility of a solo project was never his intention: 'I am part of this band and one would disrespect the other. Nevertheless, I wanted to make this music, it was in me. When you compose on the piano, you automatically get different results than on the guitar. And it was important to me to say goodbye to the realism of most Arctic Monkeys stuff. Overall, it developed in a direction that soon made me realise she had absolutely nothing to do with what people would expect from a Monkeys record.'

'(Cook's) enthusiasm has taken away my uncertainty. After a while, we brought Nick into the studio and played him our demo of Star Treatment. He was also thrilled, and so I gradually got the green light from everyone.'(cx)

Although no new music had been released, fans in attendance at the first show of their tour in San Diego were treated to a healthy chunk of new tracks, including Four Out of Five, One Point Perspective, American Sports, and She Looks Like Fun. Yet where their previous live line-up consisted of Turner, Helders, Cook, O'Malley, and Tom Rowley on keys, Tyler Parkford and Cameron Avery were brought in to bolster the sound permanently.

Elsewhere, the *NME* featured an extensive interview with Turner on the eve of the album's release, in which he revealed that he felt the lyrical style of his formative years had returned: 'I can't put my finger on exactly why I think that, but I have been saying it a lot recently. It's set in a completely different place, obviously, but there's something in the lyrics that reminds me of something in that writing. I'm tempted to say that it's something to do with how blunt it is. I think that was something I was trying to get away from, and perhaps I've returned to it now.'

This mentality is best represented in the album's opening line: 'I just wanted to be one of The Strokes, now look at the mess you made me make.' In reference to it, Turner said: '(it) does make me think about then and how much time seems to have suddenly passed. I expected to change it, but by the time I got back around to it, it seemed like it was exactly what it needed to be, and I was obviously attracted to how blunt it was.'

Elsewhere, on the day before the album's release, when interviewed by Annie Mac for Radio 1, the presenter reminded the frontman of the Ike Turner description of *AM*, to which Turner conceded that he may have 'lost something' since 2013. Across the media campaign for the album, Turner seemed less confident and more reserved than previously; the American inflections had gone from his accent, as had the flippancy, to be replaced by the more thoughtful and hesitant young man from a decade before.

<u>Album 6:</u>

Tranquility Base Hotel + Casino
Released: 11th May 2018; UK Chart Position: 1; Label: Domino
Track Listing: Star Treatment; One Point Perspective; American Sports; Tranquility Base Hotel + Casino; Golden Trunks; Four Out of Five; The World's First Ever Monster Truck Front Flip; Science Fiction; She Looks Like Fun; Batphone; The Ultracheese
Producers: James Ford and Alex Turner

As predicted by Guy Moot, thousands of people across the world awoke that Friday morning and listened to the album as one, creating a unique listening experience; alone but together. Conversation among music fans both online and in person was rife and, unsurprisingly, it received a mixed response, its otherworldly sonic palette too much of a change for some but welcomed by others. The passing of time now belies the bewildering experience of the first listen.

Tranquility Base Hotel + Casino wastes no time. The opening piano on Star Treatment, which becomes the tentpole around which the song is built, is a whole new dimension for Arctic Monkeys. The first we hear of Turner is a warble then a croon, as the opening line not only grabs the attention but is as openly autobiographical as anything he'd written, before jumbled lyrics and absurdist suave enable the song to plod along at an almost glacial, but technically mature, pace. Its near-six-minute length informs us that we're a long, long way from *AM,* in a different orbit, even.

Where the piano is often hesitant, the drums are stoic, and the woozy, almost foggy atmosphere of the song is immersive. Turner's enunciation is superb, as the lyrics verge on psychedelic while he flits in and out of character: 'Maybe I was a little too wild in the 70s, rocket-ship grease down the cracks of my knuckles.' Creating a character and a storyline, we can loosely presume that the protagonist is a lounge singer who is espousing a stream of consciousness and takes an 'elevator down to my make-believe residency,' before being told to stop drinking; 'so who you gonna call? The Martini police?' makes up the chorus, if it can be called that.

Star Treatment was written in the same

period as *Everything You've Come to Expect* in Shangri-La and the correlation is clear, the former even including another musical reference ('long hot summer,' a song by The Style Council). It successfully conjures up images of lying back and taking the world in, best exemplified by: 'as we gaze skyward, ain't it dark early?' while the faint guitars drift upwards towards the song's outro. What do you mean, you've never seen *Blade Runner*?

If any listeners were praying the piano would appear only once, its insistent use on One Point Perspective surely killed any hopes. The song's title is taken from a cinema technique used by filmmakers (most notably Stanley Kubrick), in which all lines and angles in a shot point to the character at the centre of the picture, designed to be unsettling and ominous. With another memorable opening line ('Dancing in my underpants, I'm gonna run for government,'), One Point Perspective contains a solid chord progression that ups the stakes when required.

It includes the album's first sing-along moment: 'I've been driving around listening to the score,' fits while Turner describes 'Singsong 'Round the Money Tree", this stunning documentary that no one else unfortunately saw.' The wired guitar is the top layer of a track containing organs and strings that only present themselves upon repeated listens before segueing into the next song.

Turner readily admitted that he opted to remove the confines of starting and finishing a story within a song and would instead allude to elements and themes more obliquely. Nowhere on the album is this better represented than on American Sports, which takes snippets of social observations and allows the listener to fill in the blanks.

'Breaking news, they take the truth and make

it fluid,' can only be a response to the rise of 'Fake News' from 2015 onwards, associated with then-US President Donald Trump who, when not liking the content or description in a news story, would use the phrase as a catch-all moniker. 'The trainer's explanation was accepted by the steward,' is a more loaded line, (provided by Turner's grandfather upon watching a steward's inquiry during horse racing) invoking ideas of officials or those in power accepting an answer that either makes their lives easier or suits their narrative, rather than being the truth of the matter.

The rise of populist leaders and ideas in the latter half of the 2010s (such as Trump, Brazilian President Jair Bolsonaro, or the Brexit movement in the UK) unveiled increased polarisation within societies as well as attempts to discredit the media to turn voters against institutions and long-held establishments. Lies became currency and it soon became clear that these ideas were tapping into deep resentments certain corners of society held, mostly against immigrants (a historically easy target) while at the same time offering simple, easy-to-comprehend (if impossible) solutions such as 'Make America Great Again,' or 'Take Back Control'.

American Sports hints at the changing social habits of being fed 'fake news' through technology ('Emergency battery pack just in time for my weekly chat with God on video call,') and carries a post-apocalyptic air through an eerie keyboard line. Covering commercialisation and the profit-and-loss society we inhabit at present; it bristles with ideas and metaphors which Turner leaves to the listener's interpretation.

Cleverly, his delivery of the line, 'And I never thought, not in a million year, that I'd meet so many

Lolas,' is such that the last word appears to be 'lovers' further throwing open the route to interpretation, as well as betraying his Sheffield accent. Lola is most famously a song by The Kinks, with the song's titular character being a cross-dresser. Perhaps Turner is alluding to the changes in gender stereotypes over the last few years.

American Sports apparently sounded best on Turner's dusty Tascam and the demo had a charm difficult to replace, so he and his fellow musicians decided not to try and instead built upon it, with Tyler Parkford's meaningful piano complementing Helders' subtle but important drumming. The middle eight re-establishes the science-fiction tone, Turner sounding as if he's communicating across space. At less than three minutes, it's an unheralded gem.

The album's overarching theme, or more specifically its location, returns (obviously) in the spooky, stuttering title track, a reference to both the site of the first moon landing in 1969 and the name given to Turner's piano room (Lunar Base). It feels suitably futuristic, a soundtrack to a Kubrick film that never was, with pulsing electronics and a sly hero of a bassline, delivered by Turner's friends from Mini Mansions (who were on tour with Sparks during the recording sessions, explaining their choice of delivery).

Turner views the album as a collection of short stories under the umbrella of the title track, covering one character's sense of being, and within it, he inhabits the receptionist Mark ('speaking, please tell me how may I direct your call?'). Knowing what we do of the frontman, it can't be coincidence that the first verse concludes with the other use of the word mark ('But I just manage to miss the mark,') while his alternating delivery of the title line each time keeps those hoping to sing along on their toes. Indeed, as elsewhere on the album, Turner's vocal delivery is unpredictable and curious, perhaps reflecting his choice to subvert everything we knew about the band.

It reportedly comes from 'the same place' as Four Out of Five, which refers to 'lunar surface on a Saturday night,' and the 'cute new places keep on popping up around Clavius', a crater on the Moon. The Information Action Ratio, here depicted as a cocktail (or taqueria), was a concept coined by cultural critic Neil Postma, indicating the relationship between a piece of information and what action, if any, a consumer of that information may take upon learning it. The titular grading system appears to be a review of the hotel but could also refer to the way consumers are now encouraged to grade everything through their phones, such as 'liking' a comment or providing stars on TripAdvisor and other websites.

The chorus line is an advert for Tranquility Base Hotel + Casino ('take it easy for a little while, come and stay with us, it's such an easy flight,') while also betraying 'Mark's' inner thoughts: 'I'm in no position to give advice, I don't wanna be nice but you know that'. Held together by the gnarly riff and immovable drumming, as the song proceeds it begins to drown in its symphony, a faint Elizabethan music box coming into earshot, holding its own against a flood of strings and keys which threaten to drown it until the last chorus line sends back the tide. The catchiest song on the album, it was unsurprisingly selected as a single and sits well alongside the other anthems in Arctic Monkeys' canon, even if a lot more effort is required to learn the words.

Sitting on either side of Mark's travails is Golden Trunks, driven by a simple yet haunting piano line with descending/upscaling melody vocal melody from Turner. The protagonist in the story is falling for the character to whom he's singing ('And in response to what you whispered in my ear, I must admit, sometimes I fantasise about you too,') but the most infamous line is also the most blatant on the album: 'The leader of the free world reminds you of a wrestler wearing tight golden trunks.' Without question a reference to Donald Trump and his aggressive, macho style of presidency which left diplomacy at the door in favour of bravado. However, the line is delivered (in the song), by the object of the protagonist's desire, as Turner goes back and forth within their conversation without signposting who is talking.

He expands on his point of the overtly aggressive style of leadership, along with weary resignation: 'Bendable figures with a fresh new pack of lies, summat else to publicise, I'm sure you've heard about enough,', the figures who steer the news to suit their narrative and bewilder the audience being a common trait amongst populist leaders. The influence of the Beach Boys' late 1960s period is most prevalent here, with warm harmonies from those in the studio on the last chorus calling to mind The Carpenters' saccharine voices, even if Turner tries to push away from the melody rather than embracing it.

Speaking to *Billboard* of his new approach to directly addressing politics, Turner confirmed that 'in the past I've struggled to find the poetry in (politics) and I think I've managed a way to find it this time, with some encouragement. I've always thought that, writing anything that relates to politics, it's a lot to do with the way you go about it. Being able to write about the power of allusion and suggestions is important to keep in mind.'(cxv)

Side two opens with The World's First Ever Monster Truck Front Flip which, the bizarre title aside (a headline that Turner saw on TV and consequently goggled at), feels like two disparate songs fused as one. The obnoxious organ briskly accompanies a verse that culminates in a Kinksian ditty ('you push the button and we'll do the rest,') whereas the chorus is structured as a full-on, lighters-in-the-air anthem.

The title is a metaphor for mankind's evolution, as Turner admitted that the headline blew his mind, and the line, 'the exotic sound of data storage, nothing like it first thing in the morning,' represents the fetishization that we have of technology in contemporary society. The chorus meanwhile is partially oblique (who are Jeanie and Lizzy?) but the second half is a Turner classic: 'There are things that I just cannot explain to you and those that I hope I don't ever have to.'

As previously established, the influence of science fiction on the album is vast, and the song of the same name explores that idea. The genre creates other worlds in which we can explore our societal issues, with Turner admitting that, after reading certain books and watching shows such as *World On A Wire* (referenced within the lyrics) by German director Rainer Werner Fassbinder, he began to access a different sort of vocabulary which lead to the album's 'concept' emerging but, as self-aware as ever, always with an eye on pretentiousness: 'I've a feeling that the whole thing may just well end up too clever for its own good, the way some science fiction does.' The effect is a creepy, eerie song, with disgruntled guitar jazz and the mental image of a hooded figure playing the spooky organ. An intriguing curio and the first song written for the album.

After showing immense discipline to serve the songs, Matt Helders is finally allowed to unleash (albeit in a reserved way) on the comparatively frenetic She Looks Like Fun, which rollicks up and down and is the 'rockiest' track on the album. Written about the characters people create in the virtual world, or the parallel universe within their phone ('Finally there's a place where you can wag your tongue,'), it's scathing of the attitudes people adopt ('There's no limit to the length of the dickheads we can be,') given the freedom they have to lie unreservedly ('Wayne Manor, what a memorable NYE,').

Arctic Monkeys are sometimes said to be ahead of their time, an argument that can be proven in one line on She Looks Like Fun: 'No one's on the streets, we moved it all online as of March.' Less than two years after the release of *Tranquility Base Hotel + Casino,* most of the civilised world would indeed be living their lives online during the COVID-19 pandemic.

Throughout the world, countries were put in lockdown, with the first of the UK's commencing in March 2020. One awaits the interviews with Alex Turner to gauge his thoughts on his frankly disturbing foreshadowing which could be a coincidence but could also explain what he does between albums: pulling the strings of the world.

Although lyrically dense, Turner's enunciation across the album is perfect, with little room for misinterpretation (although the re-emergence of his native tongue does cause some confusion). It's also the first time he allows himself to sing and accordingly goes in interesting directions such as on Batphone, where he rolls and follows the song rather than delivering a melody on top.

The song itself is another cynical view of our dependence on technology ('life became a spectator sport,') built from the line: 'I launch my fragrance called "Integrity". Turner later confirmed that he visualised the font on a perfume bottle then built outwards. The sparse, plodding beat is interspersed with a woozy Western guitar which drifts in, out, and upwards while the rest of the musicians are almost hesitant in keeping up with it, yet its placing on the album does feel like a false ending.

We are treated to a definitive ending straight afterward, however. The Ultracheese could even be a summary of Arctic Monkeys' whole career, as Turner ruminates on how he has 'still got pictures of friends on the wall, I suppose we aren't really friends anymore,' surely referring to people within the band's orbit that came and went, as happens to all humans. Elsewhere, he summarises many of the album's themes and influences on this big-show, *Ziggy Stardust*-era Bowie-flecked track, which features each of the album's contributors.

The changes in behaviour that technology has affected ('Got freaked out by a knock at the door when I haven't been expecting one and didn't that used to be part of the fun once upon a time?'), modern politics ('trust the politics to come along,'), semi-autobiography ('dress like a fictional character,'), science fiction ('when you were just trying to orbit the sun,') and even creation itself ('It stays between us, Steinway and his sons,') are all referenced in a neat epilogue to the biggest creative risk of Arctic Monkeys' career.

The lounge pop shocked and appalled the mainstream fan at first, as it became clear that *Tranquility Base Hotel + Casino* was going to require some effort. After the initial surprise at their frequency of use, the pianos became wearing but have grown to be appreciated as the vital component of the album. But in 2018, it was quite a sight to see people collectively lose their minds or react with incredulity. While guitar and drums were used sparingly but effectively, Nick O'Malley excels with always-interesting bass contributions. If indeed it is O'Malley on bass at all points, as the group threw everything up in the air, refusing to constrain themselves to their regular positions.

As well as being inspired by the works of French director Jean-Pierre Melville, the Tascam 388 tape recorder became the centre of Turner's musical universe and was a key element in this hybrid of dusty demos and full band arrangements, building the song from the skeleton of the original 8-track demo. The common perception of the album, then as now, is that it was a complete about-turn from the group which, when compared with *AM*, it was, but there's a clear throughline from *Everything You've Come to Expect* and *Belladonna of Sadness,* in the musicianship and slightly more oblique song style. Alex Turner pushed the method, after familiarising himself with it via his contributions to those two albums, into off-kilter and new directions.

It was later revealed that the dedication in the inner sleeve (For Tootus), was dedicated to a faithful dog, with one of the many confounding mysteries of the album solved. *Tranquility Base Hotel + Casino* cemented the perception that Turner and his bandmates sit in a rock star tradition of old: pushing themselves into new areas and following their muse, as opposed to delivering the same format album after album.

The front cover was a scaled model of the

titular hotel and casino which Turner himself created as a visual aid to his ideas. His diligence was so all-encompassing that the record which plays beneath the model is a test pressing of the album itself. 'I was going to the art-supply store quite often. I became quite consumed by that,' he told *Rolling Stone.* 'Getting up in the middle of the night, going down and delving in. I kept calling it the lobby model, like the idea that sometimes those things sit in the lobbies of the buildings they represent – that loop is appealing to me, like in *The Shining,* with the miniature hedge maze in the lobby, and he's looking in there and he sees the people are in there...'(cxvi)

The reviews for the album were largely positive, praising its ambition. *NME* best conveyed the feelings of most: 'At first it's completely overwhelming – you'll be trying to connect the scattered dots on this initially impenetrable listen, and maybe even despairing when it doesn't all come together. But when the constellations show through, you'll realise that it's a product of searingly intelligent design.'(cxi) *Pitchfork* declared that Turner had 'regenerated Arctic Monkeys in service of a delirious and artful satire directed at the foundations of modern society,'(cxii) while *The Guardian* acknowledged that 'there is a risk that this atmospheric record, one that wrong-foots expectation, might not land well. But this voyage into themed purgatory....is worth it.'(cxiii)

Not that it mattered; their ongoing success had guaranteed that Arctic Monkeys were critic-proof and, with combined sales of 86,000 in its first week, *Tranquility Base Hotel + Casino* hit the number 1 spot in the UK. The single release of Four Out of Five ostensibly followed three days later and made the top 20, while Star Treatment and One Point Perspective hit number 23 and 26 respectively. Interestingly, considering single releases are also based on streams, their placing suggests that many listeners abandoned the group's new dimension after the first two songs on the album.

UK Album Chart – Top 10 – 18th May 2018:

1. ***Tranquility Base Hotel + Casino* – Arctic Monkeys**
2. *The Greatest Showmen* – Motion Picture Cast Recording
3. *Beerbongs & Bentleys* – Post Malone
4. *Voicenotes* – Charlie Puth
5. *Staying At Tamara's* – George Ezra
6. *Divide* – Ed Sheeran
7. *Speak Your Mind* – Anne-Marie
8. *Dua Lipa* – Dua Lipa
9. *Invasion Of Privacy* – Cardi B
10. *The Prodigal Son* – Ry Cooder

Single 21:

Four Out of Five
Released: 13th May 2018; UK Chart Position: 18; Label: Domino; Album: *Tranquility Base Hotel + Casino*
Producers: James Ford and Alex Turner

UK Singles Chart – Top 10 – 18th May 2018:

1. One Kiss – Calvin Harris & Dua Lipa
2. Nice For What – Drake
3. No Tears Left to Cry – Ariana Grande
4. Freaky Friday – Lil Dicky ft Chris Brown

5. 2002 – Anne-Marie
6. This Is America – Childish Gambino
7. Answerphone – Banx & Ranx/Ella Eyre/Bane
8. Paradise – George Ezra
9. Flames – David Guetta ft Sia
10. In My Blood – Shawn Mendes

....

18. Four Out of Five – Arctic Monkeys

The Four Out of Five video was filmed at Castle Howard in the band's native Yorkshire, featuring two versions of Turner, one as a director in a white jacket filming package videos for the Tranquility Base Hotel + Casino itself. Clearly in homage to Stanley Kubrick (as directors Ben Chappell and Aaron Brown acknowledged), a second version of Turner, clad in a black suit, joins the band for the song's climax while his counterpart watches on, having been filmed walking through Munich Marienplatz station.

One shot shows the white-jacketed Turner (with a goatee) driving a car with a ghost in the back seat, representing one version talking to the other, an idea of the frontman's which enabled Chappell to immediately recognise the direction in which he was going. Chappell also took the photographs for the album during the band's time at La Frette.

With so much of the album based around Turner's demos, questions were raised as to why he had opted not to release a solo album. When asked by *The Sunday Times*, he responded: 'I enjoy their (his bandmates') company. So, for instance, on this project I was really unsure about what I was doing and lost it completely. Then, when Jamie came out to LA to join me and we worked on stuff together, through his encouragement suddenly I felt completely different...(Cook) getting excited about it, like the way I remember him getting excited about some idea in his bedroom in his mum's house when we were 16...I still get a buzz out of his reaction.'(cxiv)

Noticing the political points made on *Tranquility Base Hotel + Casino* became a trend in the post-release interviews in which Turner engaged. 'I'd never wanted anything political to get into the music and that was because I didn't know how to do it,' he told *The Sunday Times.* 'It's not as though these are protest songs necessarily, but I'm more confident about putting myself across.'

'I seem to remember feeling like I hadn't given sufficient consideration to these issues to be able to discuss them, which I'm not sure is necessarily a bad attitude towards it. They often are complex. It can go too far the other way, where people feel forced to talk about it, but they haven't given it too much thought. There is a pressure on you now to think about stuff, which is not unhealthy.' Elsewhere in the same interview, Turner addressed the Liberty tax strategy of 2014: 'we were given some poor advice and I made a poor decision. But I always paid my taxes in full, on time.'(cxvii)

After a headline slot at Primavera Sound in Barcelona, Arctic Monkeys played a special, one-off show at the Royal Albert Hall in London for the charity Warchild in early June, re-introducing From the Ritz to The Rubble to their set after a seven-year absence. In the same week, a TV special (*Arctic Monkeys Live At The BBC*) aired on BBC Two, filmed at Maida Vale studios and consisting of performances of Cornerstone, One Point Perspective, R U Mine?, Four Out of Five, I Bet You Look Good On The Dancefloor, Do I Wanna Know? and Star Treatment.

CHAPTER THIRTEEN
'I Wanna Make a Simple Point About Peace and Love, But in a Sexy Way Where It's Not Obvious' (2018-2020)

In July 2018, Arctic Monkeys performed at their only UK festival show of the year: a headline performance at TRNSMT festival in Glasgow, drawing upon tracks from their entire career and with the mandatory appearance by Miles Kane for 505.

The setlist was:

Four Out of Five
Brianstorm
Don't Sit Down 'Cause I've Moved Your Chair
The View from The Afternoon
Arabella
Crying Lightning
Do Me A Favour
Teddy Picker
Why'd You Only Call Me When You're High?
Knee Socks
Tranquility Base Hotel + Casino
One Point Perspective
Do I Wanna Know?
Pretty Visitors
Cornerstone
I Bet You Look Good on The Dancefloor
505
Star Treatment
From the Ritz to the Rubble
R U Mine?

Amusingly, Alex Turner's appearance continued to receive as much attention from fans as his band's music. After a petition for Turner to remove his beard had fallen on deaf ears some months previously, the singer had another shock in store. Appearing on *The Late Show with Stephen Colbert* in the US, he unveiled a new hairstyle, replacing his near-shoulder length hair with a buzzcut. Seemingly of less importance was that the group performed The Ultracheese on the show. Meanwhile, the title track was selected as the second single from *Tranquility Base Hotel + Casino.*

Single 22:

Tranquility Base Hotel + Casino
Released: 23rd July 2018; UK Chart Position: N/A; Label: Domino; Album: *Tranquility Base Hotel + Casino*
B-Side: Anyways
Producers: James Ford and Alex Turner

Shot at the Peppermill Reno hotel in Reno, Nevada, the video featured the same Stanley Kubrick-inspired visual style as the Four Out Of Five clip, with Turner living in the titular hotel and casino, travelling around the floors, and lounging in the leisure facilities. He also plays the role of 'Mark', even answering one call on the Batphone as he sat in the Batmobile from the 1960s version of *Batman,* starring Adam West.

Unlike the previous single, Tranquility Base Hotel + Casino included a B-side with its physical release in November 2018. Anyways was recorded separately from the other songs of the period, with all instruments (guitar, bass, keys, and organ) played by Turner. Like the songs from the parent album, Anyways uses metaphors and allegories to render the lyrics almost impenetrable, although it does seem to be about cultural and age divides considering recent political movements.

'Putting a world to rights with Bing Crosby eyes, oversharing and its bitter aftertaste,' could be a reference to the regressive policies of Donald Trump, while it has a British equivalent in 'listening to the Shipping Forecast, driving to the airport, me and the guys, Metropolis ablaze in the rear-view, devising methods to both have and eat your cake,' potentially a reference to the falsehoods promised in the lead-up to the 2016 EU Referendum. Between those lines, Turner also references himself: 'You can call me Alexander, it's nice to meet you all.'

Arctic Monkeys embarked on the US leg of their tour in August 2018 and, in keeping with going full circle, covered The Strokes (Is This It) and The White Stripes (The Union Forever) in New York and Detroit, respectively. Elsewhere, Turner and Matt Helders discussed the polarising reaction to their sixth album in an interview with Beats 1 host Matt Wilkinson: 'I've never found much use in reading the reviews, like in either direction – if it's good or bad,'(cxviii) said Helders. Turner meanwhile suggested that the next album wouldn't take as long as *Tranquility Base Hotel + Casino* had.

In the same interview, the pair were asked about the possibility of making music towards the end of their lives, to which Helders frankly replied: 'I don't know if I can play drums like this in 40 years time,' while Turner was more optimistic: 'I like the idea that I'd be making music, whether we'd be playing those tunes or not.'(cxix)

Having spent the summer of 2018 playing gigs across Europe and North America, and with only two UK shows to their name so far, Arctic Monkeys made up for lost time in their homeland in September with a string of arena shows: two nights each at the Manchester and Birmingham arenas, two shows at the Metro Radio Arena in Newcastle, a staggering four dates each at the o2 in London and the FlyDSA Arena in Sheffield, as well as two gigs at the 3Arena in Dublin. Across the concerts they treated fans to songs not included in their recent sets, including Fluorescent Adolescent, Mardy Bum, Dancing Shoes, and A Certain Romance, while John Cooper Clarke joined the group onstage for a recitation of I Wanna Be Yours in Sheffield.

In October, the tour headed back to North America and, in an interview with *BeatRoute*, Alex Turner revealed that, so far had the band travelled in their career that playing early material felt increasingly distant: 'It feels like we're doing a cover or something when we play the first album, really. But that's fine. I don't hate doing that. It's just come to the point where I play Mardy Bum or something like that and it doesn't even feel like mine anymore.'(cxx)

Meanwhile, Matt Helders was broached on the idea of a solo album: 'I don't want to do it too soon and then regret it, like 'Oh, I shouldn't have made that kind of record,' he told podcast *The Trap.* 'I think I'm getting to a point now in which the style has developed and what I want to do is more clear to me than it was before…I will do it. It's like figuring out why as well...I just like the process of creating it.'

'Maybe it's more because I'm not writing the lyrics, so it's fine that I do that. When you're writing a record and you're putting yourself out there, a lot of people need a reason to want to hear a 'message' or 'hear my opinion on this.' That's why I'm not that interested in the lyrics side of it yet.'(cxxi) The drummer revealed the album would be electronic rather than the band music he was known for and also offered his production skills to the debut solo album by Milburn frontman (and long-time friend) Joe Carnell.

To further confuse the single release of Tranquility Base Hotel + Casino, Anyways wasn't officially announced as the B-side until October, with the release the following month. Alongside it came *Warp Speed Chic,* a 12-minute documentary directed by Ben Chappell, which documented the recording process of the album in September 2017. A successful, if much shorter (albeit still of 90 dates), album tour went to Oceania in early 2019 before wrapping up in Latin America in April, just as the Helders-produced Good Cop Bad Cop (the eventual name for Joe Carnall's project, featuring additional instrumentation and backing vocals from the drummer) released their self-titled electronic-driven debut album in late March.

The album itself received little fanfare upon its release, despite the combination of talents involved. It's a solid if unspectacular piece of work that deserves more recognition. The sombre electronica of When You're Not Winning works well, as does the chirpy and pointed Sharp Shooter. The two-part End of Level Boss is pleasant, although the driving momentum of Pt II is superior. Times New Roman has a lurching melody that is reminiscent of Arctic Monkeys, and Matt Helders' inimitable backing vocals pepper the whole album. Overall *Good Cop Bad Cop* runs out of steam and is a bit lightweight, but it will be interesting to measure it against Helders' debut album (when it eventually arrives).

Meanwhile, after dabbling in collaborative efforts such as Mongrel, former bassist Andy Nicholson launched the next stage in his career in June 2019. Rebranded as Goldteeth, he opted to stay away from the microphone and instead left vocal duties to Hannah Yadi, with whom he collaborated 50/50 on the lyrics for a self-titled debut EP and stand-alone single (Leaving) later in the year.

Although classified as R&B/rap, the EP was more in the vein of electronic pop, with Nicholson writing all the music himself. In an interview with *NME* to launch the project, Nicholson revealed: 'This project came about towards the end of last year. My daughter was born in December, and before then I was just in the studio thinking that I might not get as much time in there as I had before so I just knuckled down.

'The first song I made was actually (first single) Doin' Better, just as this random instrumental. At that point I was just like, 'This feels that it could be something on its own. This could be the start of a project that I just do by myself.' I loved it. I decided I was going to do all of the writing, recording, producing, mixing, artwork, and take as much control as possible.'

'That's what sets it apart – it's all mine, I'm making every decision and I've got to take the credit for everything; whether it's good or bad. It's all me so if everyone hates it then it's all my fault, and if everyone loves it then that's my fault too. Hopefully they will.'(cxxii) In the same interview, Nicholson disclosed that all issues with the members of his former band had been resolved and that they would speak intermittently, or when they were all in Sheffield.

Two further singles (Once I Got Away from You Then Everything Worked Out and Thinking) landed in 2020, with vocals provided by Murkage Dave and Joel Culpepper, respectively, followed by another brace in 2021 entitled Trips (featuring Piers James) and Feeling the Love. The releases continued in 2022: two EPs, *MTMT* and *This Too Shall Pass,* as well as single My Dogs Don't Bite.

After a short video (*Live in Mexico*), directed by Ben Chappell, was released online to officially mark the end of the sixth album era, speculation turned to the future for Arctic Monkeys. After such a long break between the last two albums, there was much speculation in the press that this would become a new pattern for the group, rather than the comparatively consistent nature in which they had released material during the first phase of their career.

That was the intention of the band too, with tentative plans to use the energy from the tour to write a song which would spur the next stage of their career in the same way R U Mine? had several years before. More specifically, Alex Turner wanted to write a song that would be a good contender to close their shows, and so the band decamped to La Frette to record something in that vein. Sadly, the sessions were fruitless, with only a semblance of a track, later to become Hello You, surviving.

Before the end of their world tour, Matt Helders spoke to *Musicweek* and confirmed they had no intention of having another lengthy break between albums: 'I think that break was based on various circumstances and that was sort of what we needed at the time. But it's not a pattern we're going to get used to as a band. We like being in the studio. We're keen on making albums.'(cxxxiii) As it would transpire, there would prove to be another significant gap between albums six and seven, albeit one which had to factor in the COVID-19 pandemic.

CHAPTER FOURTEEN
'No-One's on the Streets, We Moved it All Online as of March.' (2020-2022)

After the sessions to write new material fell away, Alex Turner retreated to Lunar Surface in 2020 to write but, despite his best intentions, still drew little inspiration from the guitar, as he told Keith Cameron in an interview for *Mojo*: 'I remember trying to write riffs and stuff, make it louder, but it just wasn't...it didn't want to go there.' Back then, to the Steinway piano, which eventually yielded a piano-based song which the songwriter instinctively knew was the starting point for their next album.

Before the first lockdown, Arctic Monkeys' biggest cheerleaders *NME* awarded *AM* their Album of The Decade at their 2020 Awards, although, given the praise that had been heaped upon the album by the magazine, few other albums stood a chance. Otherwise, the pandemic and worldwide lockdowns meant that all plans were thrown into disarray and if Arctic Monkeys had planned to work on new material in 2020, those ideas were shelved. Not that the most secretive band in the world would ever disclose such details.

A bone was thrown to fans in October when a photograph of Matt Helders in a recording studio was published on Instagram by photographer Andreas Neumann. That aside, not a peep of news about recordings was heard, as Alex Turner beavered away on new material primarily in isolation but with infrequent writing sessions (when restrictions allowed) with Cook and Tom Rowley, the enforced extra time allowing Turner to craft and hone his new batch of songs.

Yet there was some activity in 2020, albeit for an unwelcome cause. With no gigs allowed for an indeterminable period, music venues across the world were left in financial peril as no shows meant no audience and no income. Although the larger venues were, by this point, owned by corporations (such as o2), the grassroots pubs etc, had no such cushion and it soon became apparent that help would be needed. Facilitated by the Music Venue Trust, a campaign to provide financial support for these small businesses was launched (#SaveOurVenues), ensuring the buildings were ready to be filled when restrictions were lifted.

In addition, a specific campaign (with donations via Crowdfunder) for The Leadmill in Sheffield, which had played host to a wealth of now world-famous acts including Coldplay, Arcade Fire, Oasis, and, of course, Arctic Monkeys, was launched. For a £5 donation, entrants had the chance to win a black Fender Stratocaster guitar donated by Alex Turner who, as always, preferred to let actions speak louder than words. The famous building was eventually granted a reprieve, with the auction raising £128,544, enabling them to pay their bills for a period. In addition, the entrants were given access to an exclusive viewing of the band's 2006 performance at the Reading Festival.

The Leadmill's general manager, Rebecca Walker, was understandably effervescent in her praise of the group, telling *NME:* 'We are so humbled and so grateful. We couldn't thank the guys enough for listening to us and allowing us to reach out to them, but also just their generosity. To them, it's just a guitar but to us it's a lifeline – it's a matter of whether a venue can stay open or not.'

'Everyone in Sheffield knows someone who knows someone who knows Arctic Monkeys. You can't go very far in the city without someone having a story about them. I happen to know someone with a connection to them so we reached out back in April and then their management said, 'We've actually been speaking with them and they were asking about you guys to see if you were alright.' It was so great to know that no matter how big they get or where they are in the world, they're still concerned with the crisis of how venues are doing back home. They were only too happy to help.'(cxxiv)

It wasn't the only (public) charitable act the group performed during that traumatic year. In October, Arctic Monkeys announced a brand-new live album: *Live at The Royal Albert Hall,* a recording of their 2018 show at the historic London venue. The band released a statement alongside an album trailer:

'On June 7 2018 we played a special show at London's Royal Albert Hall. All proceeds from that night were donated to War Child in support of the vital work they do protecting, educating & rehabilitating children who have experienced the trauma of conflict and the horror of war.

The situation that was bad in 2018 is now desperate and those children and their families need our help more than ever.

To enable War Child to reduce their funding deficit and continue their valuable work, we are releasing a live album recorded on that evening. All proceeds will go direct to the charity.'

Live Album 2:

Live At the Royal Albert Hall
Released: 4th December 2020; UK Chart Position: 3; Label: Domino
Track Listing: Four Out of Five; Brianstorm; Crying Lightning; Do I Wanna Know?; Why'd You Only Call Me When You're High?; 505; One Point Perspective; Do Me A Favour; Cornerstone; Knee Socks; Arabella; Tranquility Base Hotel + Casino; She Looks Like Fun; From the Ritz to the Rubble; Pretty Visitors; Don't Sit Down 'Cause I've Moved Your Chair; I Bet You Look Good on The Dancefloor; Star Treatment; The View From The Afternoon; R U Mine?
All lyrics by Alex Turner; all music by Arctic Monkeys

As a balm for gig-starved music fans in late 2020, *Live at the Royal Albert Hall* was bittersweet, the crowd noise a reminder of just how much live performances were missed. But otherwise, the album was a good reflection of the most recent version of Arctic Monkeys. The core band had been bolstered by the inclusion of Tom Rowley (guitar, keyboards, lap steel, and backing vocals), Tyler Parkford (keyboards, backing vocals), Scott Gillies (acoustic guitar on Four Out Of Five), Cameron Avery (acoustic guitar, keyboards, and backing vocals) and Davey Latter (percussion), who all finally received credit for their contributions.

A show that spanned the entirety of their career, the album highlights how little the band altered with a winning formula on the live stage. Each song is delivered relatively faithfully to the recorded version, apart from a few subtle additions including an extended, bass-driven introduction to Knee Socks. The only notable differences are in Alex Turner's delivery, with the evolution to his improved enunciation apparent on some earlier tracks such as Do Me A Favour or Cornerstone.

The latter track sadly suffers as a result; his drawl makes it unwieldy which seems reckless given how beautifully and concisely the recorded version flows. In contrast, on the likes of Brianstorm and From the Ritz to The Rubble, his original scattergun delivery leaves no room to draw out the lyrics, although he does his best on I Bet You Look on The Dancefloor, which he introduces with the same words as in the original video ('don't believe the hype,') in a pleasing nod to their past.

Accompanying the live album's release was a collage video for Arabella featuring live and backstage shots taken during the *Tranquility Base Hotel + Casino* tour, which assisted *Live at the Royal Albert Hall* in achieving a very respectable Number 3 on the Album Chart in a typically busy Christmas market.

<u>UK Album Chart – Top 10 – 11th December 2020:</u>

1. *Weird* - Yungblud
2. *Together at Christmas* – Michael Ball & Alfie Boe
3. ***Live At the Royal Albert Hall* – Arctic Monkeys**
4. *Classic Diamonds* – Neil Diamond & LSO
5. *Music Played by Humans* – Gary Barlow
6. *Jolly Holiday* – Andre Rieu & Johann Strauss Or
7. *Christmas* – Michael Buble

8. *Don't Let the Devil Take Another Day* – Kelly Jones
9. *Power Up* – AC/DC
10. *Believe* – Andrea Bocelli

Although the band didn't engage in any promotion for the record, their manager Ian McAndrew spoke to *Musicweek,* revealing that, 'They're working on new music. In this rather disjointed time, the guys are beavering away and I hope that next year they'll start working on some new songs, new ideas, with a view on a future release.'

'There were recording plans in the summertime that got canned as a result of the travel restrictions.'(cxxvi) Amusingly, in the same interview, McAndrew confirmed that the group didn't interact via Zoom (as became a necessity through the pandemic) in the same spirit that they didn't engage on social media.

As 2020 became 2021, Matt Helders, contradicting his manager, confirmed in an Instagram Live chat that his group were in the preliminary stages of writing a new record but being based in various parts of the world was prohibiting them from doing much else. Meanwhile, Andy Nicholson revealed that Helders had contributed some drum tracks for a lockdown EP, while the drummer once again dipped his toe into clothes design, with a new range of *Tranquility Base Hotel + Casino* products announced in the early part of the year.

Continuing his position as the public face of the band, Matt Helders met up with internet sensation Nandi Bushell for a jam and interview. Bushell, an 11-year-old girl with extraordinary drumming talents, had managed to catch the attention of Dave Grohl, Royal Blood, and Tom Morello from Rage Against the Machine over the lockdowns, but her meeting with Helders was her first 'in-person' collaboration.

With Helders behind the drum kit, Bushell released three videos of jams (I Bet You Look Good on The Dancefloor, Brianstorm, and R U Mine?) as well as a long interview with the drummer in which he informed the youngster that, to no great surprise, Brianstorm was the song he found most difficult to play.

All COVID-related restrictions were eventually lifted in the UK by July 2021, with a staggered approach to gatherings meaning that Arctic Monkeys were finally able to convene at Butley Priory in Suffolk (although, being based in LA, Matt Helders had to isolate for several days upon arrival in the UK). Primarily used as a wedding venue but capable of fulfilling the functions of a recording studio, they commenced the recording of their seventh album with James Ford back at the helm. The producer was familiar with the venue having celebrated his 40th birthday there, while Rowley and Loren Humphrey were assigned engineering duties.

Further sessions, or 'the edit' (as Turner would late come to recall them), took place at La Frette and RAK studios in London with vocals, overdubs, and strings added to the band's work in Suffolk. Turner and Ford separately drafted string arrangements before composer Bridget Samuels edited then composed them to accompany the music thus far made.

Describing the process to Dutch radio station NPO 3FM the following year, Turner said: 'It's (Butley Priory) a big open room so it's got that sound. We captured the raw material there and then went back to La Frette. We did the vocals and overdubs there, with strings mixed in London, but we got the band stuff in this room in the countryside in England, in the summer. I think that was the first time we've made a record in the summer in England since the first one, so it was that approach that appealed, maybe.'

As had been the case on the previous album, Turner found inspiration not just through music but also film, citing the book *In the Blink of An Eye* by film editor Walter Murch, the triple Academy Award-winning editor of films including *The Godfather*, as he explained to *The Big Issue* in 2022: 'He was the editor on *Apocalypse Now* and a bunch of other cool stuff. It's a short book about editing. But the way he puts it across there goes way beyond that. There's a bunch of interesting ideas that he's speaking about. And that feels connected to the process and also the feel or lyrics on this new record.'

'Butley Priory was more like the shoot and then the other stuff (additional recording sessions) was like the edit. The way Walter Murch describes the edit in this book – he talks about meeting some friends of his wife and one of them says, 'So you're the guy who cuts out all the bad bits, then?' Initially he is offended, but after all these years, he came around to thinking: 'Well yeah, that is actually what I'm doing.' But the question is what constitutes a bad bit...'

'There's a great bit where he's talking about the discovery of a path through all this material that you have, and how there's a million different ways to get through it. That feels more like the way this record was put together, perhaps. More than other records I've done in the past.'

In the same interview, elaborating on how the

strings were completed, Turner expressed his enthusiasm for Samuels and her work: 'James and I came up with the melodies. You can write it on the piano and hear the melodies in your head the same way I would hear a vocal melody. Sometimes that's how you'll write a keyboard or a guitar line. But there's definitely a dimension that you get from real strings playing together that can't be emulated with anything else. Which is magic.'

'I think we've got closer to a better version of a more dynamic overall sound with this record. The strings on this record come in and out of focus, and that was a deliberate move and hopefully everything has its own space. There's times the band come to the front and then the strings come to the front.'(cxvii)

Although they were trying to keep things quiet, a photograph found its way to Instagram in summer 2021 of the band at Butley Priory while Matt Helders, speaking to the BBC in November, confirmed that the album was 'pretty much finished.' The drummer also teased the sound of the record: 'We tend to always move it on a little bit. For us, because we're so involved in it, it always makes sense. They always kind of pick up where the other one left off in a way. It makes sense when you think about it in the context of the last record. But we always try and do something different – it's kind of hard to describe. You can tell it's the same band.'(cxxviii)

In a later interview as part of DrumathonLIVE 2022, Helders broke the hearts of everyone born after 1992 in one sentence: 'It's never gonna be like R U Mine? and all that stuff again, you know, the heavy riffs and stuff. But there are riffs in there and (it's) a bit more up-tempo, even though it's not loud.'(cxxix)

Desperate fans would have to wait the better of a year to hear new material, but the wheels were set in motion in November as Arctic Monkeys announced some live shows for August 2022, in Istanbul, Burgas, Pula, and Prague, before they confirmed their third headline slot at Reading & Leeds Festival. More worldwide dates were announced in the early months of 2022, but no further information about their next stage was forthcoming.

They did, however, put their heads above the social-media parapet to declare their support for The Leadmill once again, the venue this time under threat by an eviction notice from their proprietor. The Brixton-based Electric Group, having purchased the property in 2017, declared their intentions to sustain the building as a music venue, but under a new name and new management. Meanwhile, Matt Helders was announced to be a contributor to country singer Nikki Lane's album *Denim & Diamonds,* which was produced by Josh Homme which perhaps explained his involvement.

Elsewhere, a playlist appeared on Spotify with the compiler going by Del Schwartz (a name that would soon become familiar), which included primarily instrumental pieces from the likes of Pierre Bachelet, Johanna Shimkus, and Jean-Claude Vannier as well as How Can You Say it by Gloria Ann Taylor, a song which starts in a wilder different place to where it ends up, later cited as a key methodology by Turner. Although it had little fanfare at the time, when quizzed about the playlist in a later interview, he was knowingly coy about its existence. As before, it was likely a method for Turner to highlight some of the influences on the new album without having to undertake the rigmarole of an interview to confirm as much.

CHAPTER FIFTEEN
'Puncturing Your Bubble of Relatability With Your Horrible New Sound' (2022)

Arctic Monkeys made their return in August 2022, firstly with a comeback show in Istanbul, complete with a mirror ball backdrop and Tom Rowley on additional keys and guitar, Tyler Parkford on synths, and Davey Latter once again on percussion and tambourine. But, to the chagrin of much of the internet, they resisted debuting any new material, instead focussing on a career-spanning set full of the old favourites and some surprises: Library Pictures, Fireside, That's Where You're Wrong, No. 1 Party Anthem and Potion Approaching all found their way into the sets, which were varied across their first few dates.

The drip-feed approach to the new album campaign began to become clear, and at the Zurich show the crowd was finally treated to a new song: the funk influenced I Ain't Quite Where I Think I Am which, if nothing else, reassured certain fans with Alex Turner back on electric guitar. Then, on 24th August, Arctic Monkeys announced their new album: *The Car*. Rather than making media appearances or releasing a new single from nowhere, the announcements were made through independent record shops listing the new album, while their comeback interview was an exclusive in *The Big Issue*.

The interview (with actor Martin Compston) focussed on the creative process in general, how their respective lives had changed, and their backgrounds, rather than the new album. But it did contain a few titbits of information, with Turner revealing that 'on this record, sci-f is off the table. We are back to earth.'

'...it's about everything having its own space and not all shouting at once. There is room to use all the things from the factory. And there are times I've used the wrong tool for the job, probably. But you learn from that. This time, we've kept more of an eye on the performance.'(cxxx)

And the performances kept coming, with their return to UK shores over the August bank holiday weekend. On-site, despite a heavyweight line-up on Saturday at Reading (Wolf Alice, Fontaines D.C.), Arctic Monkeys was the name on everyone's lips, with anticipation for their return at a high as they walked on stage to what was surely a record crowd for the historic festival. The mirror ball adorned the top of the stage while the big screens and circular video backdrop were sepia-tinged in a retro style, aesthetically like the *Tranquility Base* era.

After a gargantuan Do I Wanna Know? (With the crowd singing the chords as loudly as the lyrics), Turner greeted the audience with 'Hello, Reading!' spoken like an old friend, which of course the festival was. Their performance was watertight, a straight-forward yet crowd-pleasing set with minimal adjustments; Crying Lightning was embellished with extra keys on the breakdown before the final chorus, while Knee Socks was given a bluesy introduction and a garage rock outro, not wholly different from their earliest days.

Alex Turner kept crowd interaction to a minimum with a few exceptions (concisely saying 'square one,' before The View from The Afternoon) demonstrating his proficiency on guitar when required, such as adding arpeggio to Teddy Picker, or defaulting to a more restrained version of the performer of old when (without the instrument) on Cornerstone and Arabella.

On a breathless From the Ritz to the Rubble he and Cook rolled back the years, laughing and smiling as they ripped furiously through the 2004 song, before bringing things up to date by continuing to 'act' the final line of Star Treatment ('bear with me man, I lost my train of thought,' then looking blank for the remainder of the song).

To the delight of a generation-spanning crowd, no era of their career was untouched (albeit only That's Where You're Wrong representing *Suck It And See*), with hits like R U Mine?, Brianstorm, and 505 (having recently undergone a rebirth through being a TikTok 'sensation') interspersed with deeper cuts such as Potion Approaching. A masterclass of a headline set and, as a reminder of the story so far, the shows were an enormous success. All decks cleared, it was time for the new era to begin and, just over 24 hours after they left the stage at Leeds, Arctic Monkeys released their next single.

Single 23:

There'd Better Be a Mirrorball
Released: 29th August 2022; UK Chart Position: 26;
Label: Domino; Album: *The Car*
Producer: James Ford

There'd Better Be a Mirrorball commences with a slow, luxurious, circular piano before stabbed keys and a pregnant pause give way to the opening verse. Matt Helders keeps steady time on the cymbal around the intermittent piano while the hypnotic harpsichord is minimally and woozily sustained, with

Nick O'Malley's muted bass underpinning the entire song. Then, as the second chorus commences, in sweep the Scott Walker-style strings which dominate the remainder of the song, reflecting Alex Turner's mournful, falsetto-enhanced vocal delivery.

At surface level, the lyrics appear to cover either a doomed relationship, or a reluctance on the part of the main protagonist to venture out into the evening. However, as we know by now, nothing Alex Turner writes should be taken at face value and, if anything, this may have been a direct instruction to the fans of his band to manage their expectations. Surely very aware of the desire of certain corners of the fanbase for his band to return to riff-heavy rock, Turner croons, 'Yesterday's still leaking through the roof, that's nothing new,' as if to cast the past as an albatross around his neck.

The songwriter would later admit to being amused at the thought of the line as a message to fans of the group, but it's more likely to be an instruction to himself. 'I know I promised this is what I wouldn't do but somehow giving it the old romantic fool seems to better suit the mood,' indicates that, although he had planned to move elsewhere, the music he's choosing to write needs lyrics to reflect it and he followed the muse as inspired by this song as a pathway to the album.

'You're getting cynical and that won't do, I'd throw the rose tint back on the exploded view,' could be a plea not to let these negative opinions affect the listener's view of their past material; they'll always have it, even if it's gone. Being walked 'to the car' may represent any reluctance Turner (or the character he is playing) has to look back but is reassured by the presence of a mirror ball, like the one adorning their stage at the time.

Perhaps Turner (semi-autobiographically) knows 'he' is getting increasingly distant from the person who is required to perform live but must do so out of duty and necessity. Turner informed Jazz Monroe in an interview with *The Guardian* that 'before the words even come in, that instrumental piece (establishes) the feel of the record. All right...this feels like how the next record starts.'(cxxxi)

A song to bathe inside and lose oneself in, with a video directed by the frontman himself. Shot by frequent collaborators Zackery Michael, Ben Chappell, and Mark Bull, it featured images of the band recording the track taken in the summer of 2021 at Butley Priory and La Frette. Although the single didn't trouble the top 10, it still managed a respectable 26, a stark contrast to most other indie/rock bands of their era who very rarely troubled the charts in the 2020s.

UK Singles Chart – Top 10 – 9th September 2022:

1. B.O.T.A. (Baddest of Them All) – Eliza Rose/Interplanetary
2. I'm Good (Blue) – David Guetta ft Bebe Rexha
3. I Ain't Worried - OneRepublic
4. Not Over Yet – KSI ft Tom Grennan
5. Late Night Talking – Harry Styles
6. Super Freaky Girl – Nicki Minaj
7. Ferrari – James Hype/Miggy Del Rosa
8. Hold Me Closer – Elton John & Britney Spears
9. Big City Life – Luude & Mattafix
10. Crazy What Love Can Do – David Guetta/Hill/Henderson

....

26. There'd Better Be a Mirrorball – Arctic Monkeys

Meanwhile, the group continued to play festival slots across the early weeks of September, while still tweaking the setlists. A special comeback show at the Kings Theatre in Brooklyn followed, where they gave live debuts to the recent single and new tracks Body Paint and Mr Schwartz. The following day, finally satisfying their patient home fans, Arctic Monkeys announced a mammoth stadium tour of the UK (their first) for summer 2023, with dates in Bristol, Coventry, Manchester, Middlesbrough, Norwich, Swansea, Southampton, London, Dublin, Glasgow and two huge hometown shows at Hillsborough Park in Sheffield, as well as a conspicuously Glastonbury-shaped hole in their schedule.

Upon their release a week later, demand for the tickets was vast and unprecedented with many fans left disappointed or having to change from their preferred destination due to lack of availability. Further large-scale European and American tour announcements followed in the preceding weeks, many of which sold out within minutes.

Single 24:

Body Paint
Released: 29th September 2022; UK Chart Position: 26; Label: Domino; Album: *The Car*
Producer: James Ford

A second single was lifted from *The Car* before There'd Better Be a Mirrorball had left the top

100. Body Paint is much more robust than its predecessor, as innocent keys emerge along with a slight snare beat, but the snappy and steady piano chords remain, although expanded to be reminiscent of Mike Garson's 1970s work with David Bowie. The strings, now clearly a key ingredient of *The Car*, arrive in the George Martin-esque second verse, before it turns on its head, with a vaudevillian mid-section of just them.

The final act of the song splits it wide open, commencing with the welcome return of gnarly guitars clanging to announce themselves, fusing with the strings for a galvanizing outro as the whole piece comes together. The scuzzy, distorted guitar timbres recall both *Abbey Road* and the Spiders from Mars, the band clearly enjoying themselves with Turner's incandescent 'ha' the icing on the cake.

The glorious coda could go on forever, but the song limits itself to just five minutes, the group having not sounded as vibrant and alive for nearly 10 years. While Turner perhaps overeggs some of the falsettos, when one is losing themselves so whole-heartedly, it's churlish to condone them for such an action.

Turner viewed this song as written from three different perspectives; the first part is inward-looking and reflective while the second section is reaching out to a protagonist that is getting further away, before the stools are kicked away and the band goes full glam throttle. Indeed, the outro was a consequence of the band finally seeing one another after such a long time apart and unleashing in the studio.

Lyrically, while on the one hand it could be about cheating within a relationship, it could also be Turner once again veering into the autobiographical, even if he is talking in the third person: as 'a master of deception and subterfuge,' (which he has often been in his lyrics), he remonstrates that, 'you've made yourself quite the bed to lie in,' namely that the protagonist has boxed himself by being too clever by half.

Yet he has sympathy and questions their well-being, observing that, 'there's something up with the wiring,' but ultimately that person (be it he or the character) is 'so predictable, I know what you're thinking,' a simple but naggingly catchy motif. Most obviously, and this is perhaps where Turner relishes in hiding beneath layers of character, he is 'keeping on my costume,' (the character) 'and calling it a writing tool,' which Turner himself readily admitted doing on *Tranquility Base Hotel + Casino* (and indeed, he referred to his persona during *AM* as a character) while the body paint is a remnant of that writing style that he (or the character), can't shake off. His ongoing games of four-dimensional chess just get more intricate.

The video, directed by Brook Linder with Ben Chappell as creative director, was filmed between London and Missouri, and is based inside an editing suite, with shots such as a man looking at a helicopter or a tanning booth, all adding elements to the 'film soundtrack' concept of the album, interspersed with the band playing. Linder uses motifs of circular motion and screens-within-screens to represent the lyrics and the imagery.

<u>UK Singles Chart – Top 10 – 13th October 2022:</u>

1. Unholy – Sam Smith & Kim Petras
2. I'm Good (Blue) – David Guetta ft Bebe Rexha

3. Forget Me – Lewis Capaldi
4. B.O.T.A. (Baddest of Them All) – Eliza Rose/Interplanetary
5. I Ain't Worried - OneRepublic
6. Celestial – Ed Sheeran
7. Super Freaky Girl – Nicki Minaj
8. Under The Influence – Chris Brown
9. Bad Habit – Steve Lacy
10. Cuff It – Beyonce

……………………………………………………

26. Body Paint – Arctic Monkeys

In contrast to the relatively muted press campaign for the previous album (certainly before its release), Arctic Monkeys hit the media hard in the lead-up to the release of *The Car*. As well as performances on *The Jimmy Fallon Show* in the US and an equivalent in the UK (*The Jonathan Ross Show*) they spoke with most major newspapers and appeared on all the alternative radio stations, ensuring a wealth of publicity in the weeks surrounding its release.

Attention that would be required; the album was going to head-to-head with US megastar Taylor Swift, releasing her tenth studio album *Midnights* on the same day as *The Car.*

Album 7:

The Car
Released: 21st October 2022; UK Chart Position: 2; Label: Domino
Track Listing: There'd Better Be a Mirrorball; I Ain't Quite Where I Think I Am; Sculptures of Anything Goes; Jet Skies on The Moat; Body Paint; The Car; Big Ideas; Hello You; Mr Schwartz; Perfect

Sense
Producer: James Ford
Sculptures of Anything Goes written by Alex Turner and Jamie Cook, Jet Skies on The Moat and Mr Schwartz written by Alex Turner and Tom Rowley

While it's reasonable to assume that Alex Turner drew inspiration from his own experiences for the rock star at the centre of *Tranquility Base Hotel + Casino*, the same (or a similar) character is almost a parallel version of him on *The Car.* They had, in their own words, just come down to earth but further layers of mystery are added as the rock star is also, seemingly, the subject of a film.

Turner gave some insight into that the theory of hiding further and further beneath characters when he spoke to *The Guardian:* 'Normally, the record you make encourages a certain style of performance. But thinking about the performer in relation to *Tranquility*, or this thing – I have considered that you can invert that. The performer can influence the music, rather than the other way around.'(cxxxiii)

After the sublime There'd Better Be a Mirrorball sets the scene, with a melancholy rock star being hauled out to perform one more time, I Ain't Quite Where I Think I Am swiftly lifts the mood. Flexing their musical muscles, the group turn their hand to funk for the first time, channelling *Young Americans*-era Bowie, the Isley Brothers, and Al Green with some succinct guitar licks and stoic drumming, before allowing the strings to dominate the song's midsection. The dalliance with the wah-wah guitar led to both this and the next song, which Turner described as the moment 'where everything clicked.'(cxxxviii)

The intermittent 'wahs' (delivered by each member of the band) never fail to surprise when they appear in the song and, although the chorus doesn't quite scan, the creeping bridge recalls their *AM* period and is therefore much more recognisable as a pop song. The group spent several months hammering the song together, its disjointed component parts needing work to ensure the song would flow.

Lyrically we're inside our hero's head, as he flitters from scenario to scenario by being at 'the retina scan' one moment then failing to 'see past the disco strobes in the stumbling blocks,' as they must 'shake a few hands' in the intermission. Such is the rock star's life: discombobulating in that they take in sights and sounds at a pace that mere mortals would struggle to comprehend, ultimately not quite being where they think they are.

Perhaps seeing 'both islands' is literal as the protagonist is travelling (in a car, for example) but, before they know it, they are at their next destination while in their head they have experienced fleeting moments only recently. I Ain't Quite Where I Think I Am was released as a single three days before the album, with a live video of the band performing at King's Theatre in New York.

The mood darkens on the chilling Sculptures of Anything Goes, some remnants of the science-fiction not completely expunged, a track that shows Arctic Monkeys at their most menacing. The result of Jamie Cook playing a drum machine through a Moog synthesizer then through a guitar pedal (his first writing credit since Still Take You Home), it reportedly went through several changes and elaborations before the group eventually settled on the original sound. It recalls some of the moodier moments of both *Favourite Worst Nightmare* and *Humbug,* specifically 505 and Pretty Visitors.

Alex Turner proposed that the sound generated by the Moog may have prompted the title; the unusual method of garnering a new sound simulating Anything Goes. New territory for the group, Sculptures of Anything Goes lurches into life like an angry Portishead, cold and industrial as the band come in and out of focus against the Moog.

Possibly the most oblique song on the album, Turner speculates that the protagonist is 'puncturing your bubble of relatability with your horrible new sound,' (which seems close to the bone given the reception to the previous album) in this venue of 'gallery walls' and 'chandeliers'. He dreams of a quieter life of 'village coffee mornings with not long since retired spies,' but also has 'performing in Spanish on Italian TV,' on his mind.

There's also space for a mum joke, which somewhat goes against the mood and vibe of the song, but otherwise it's moody and magnificent. The track is the best evidence of his group's approach to the album, as Turner told *The Guardian*: 'Rather than strings on top of rock, I was interested in switching the 'rock band' on and off. With the Sculptures song, the 'rock band' fader comes up for two bars here and there, and then it's switched back off.'(cxxxii)

More recognisable rock star terrain follows, the sexy, bubbling pop of Jet Skies on The Moat immediately evoking imagery of the high life with Turner delivering soulful vocals. Initially a composition by Tom Rowley (the musician had sent a piece of music to Turner who, upon hearing it, immediately sang the title), its's reminiscent of the solo work of John Lennon, although it perhaps outstays its welcome with a ponderous pace. Yet the musicianship is warm and comforting with swooning guitar, less obviously funky than I Ain't Quite Where I Think I Am but with equally snappy licks.

Here the cinematic themes come to the fore, as the director 'shot it all in CinemaScope as though it's the last time.' The lead character is seemingly now depressed about their circumstances ('you know it's alright if you wanna cry,') but unable to do anything apart from 'watch while the paint job dries.' All he has are his comrades in 'Showstoppers Anonymous' and a blissful unawareness that 'it' (their career?) is over.

In Turner's own words, the title track sees Arctic Monkeys going further in a specific direction than they ever have, the strings propelling the band to explore new terrain. Opening with a repeated, finger-plucked acoustic riff, it recalls Green Fields by The Good, The Bad & The Queen and has similarities to the dusty efforts on *Submarine*, but with added winding Arabian-esque guitar in the midsection. A favourite of the group to play live, the guitar tones develop throughout the song, yet it's the most enigmatic to Turner himself.

Our mysterious rock star is now having some downtime: 'it ain't a holiday until you go and fetch something from the car,' but is still cautious of the media as they sweep the apartment for bugs. In some of the press rounds for the album, Turner stated that the music (rather than the lyrics) was more autobiographical than before, and while the Mediterranean timbres fit the imagery of 'sleepy amigos' and the 'boat kiosk lady,' we know it's still our hero playing his grandfather's guitar.

The Car was written on acoustic and inspired by the album cover (a photograph taken by Matt

Helders in his LA apartment) which in turn inspired the lyrical themes of surveillance, the photograph present in Turner's head throughout. The title song is a gem and opens several avenues for the band to explore in the next stage of their evolution, such as the distant thunder of the percussion.

Much was made by music journalists of the potentially autobiographical lyrics in the reviews and interviews for the album, with Big Ideas the song that most concretely supports that theory. As has been documented, Arctic Monkeys have followed their muse and instinct throughout their career without thinking much further ahead. Or, as Turner himself said to *The Guardian*: 'The name of the band seems to allude to how limited expectations were,'(cxxxiv), but some lyrics here are so pointed that the press can be forgiven in their assumption (indeed, they may be correct, and Turner is just lying).

He may also be utilising his own experience as, although he pictures a director saying the opening lines, the line, 'can you co-direct and play the twins?' could be a reference to the Four Out of Five video in which Turner did exactly that, while the 'nationwide festivities' perhaps reference their performance at the London Olympics.

To say nothing of 'the orchestra's got me surrounded' which, given the conscious use of strings across the album, is breaking the fourth wall to such an extent that it's almost mocking. Perhaps this rock star didn't hit the heights that Turner and his group have. Regardless, he admits that some lyrical ideas that would previously have been 'shut out' are allowed to adorn the song.

Big Ideas began life with the instrumental section at the midpoint, the tune entering Turner's head which he then recorded, once he had figured out what the notes were. The piece was left for a while to create a full song around it but took so long that the music eventually influenced his lyrics, along with a melody that had aspirations beyond a pop song but was reportedly pulled back into the pop sphere by the band.

The strings create such evocative imagery and would fit perfectly as part of the score for a European movie, were it not for the distorted, Led Zeppelin-esque guitar solo which brings it back into band territory. This was intentional, as Alex Turner told *Musikexpress*: 'I like the idea that *The Car* is about this big production in the background which, with its set, is this common thread throughout the entire record. I can't even tell you what type of production it is, but it gives this record a base from which we can operate from.'(cxxxvi)

The oldest song on the album, Hello You was initially written in their 2019 sessions after the *Tranquility Base Hotel + Casino* tour, but only the piano section made the final cut on the final, Quincy Jones-esque song, which was for some time omitted but found its way back onto the album. While slightly jaunty, the strings and percussion have a forward motion that complements Turner's falsetto well, even if the former is reminiscent of John Coltrane's Love Supreme.

The opening line ('Lego Napoleon movie written in gas-filled glass tubes underlined in sparks,') is Turner imagining the *Lego Movie* team taking an unrealised script by Stanley Kubrick about the French Emperor and adding it to their franchise, using the notion as an idea about *having* ideas. Self-aware as ever, he follows it with: 'I'll admit it's elaborate for a waking thought,' and admitted to Zane Lowe on Apple Music that some of the lyrics recall 'that point in the night where you're waffling.'

We know better than that, of course, and it's clear to see why this track was so important in the development of the album, with references to 'overtaking the tractor,' and 'picking your moment along a country lane,' cementing the metaphors and symbolism of the titular car. Rawborough Snooker Club is a reference to the 1985 film *Tread Softly Stranger,* a film which Turner admits to not having seen, but an important film for his grandfather. It's also the second reference to the film in his lyrics after citing the title in The Jeweller's Hands, while the semi-autobiographical theme returns as Turner believes he could 'pass for seventeen if I just get a shave and catch some Zzz.'

Turner referred to the idea of how moments come and go in a flash while having the power to resonate later in life when speaking to *The Big Issue:* 'Maybe that's barking up that tree a little. Well, a lot. I'm thinking about going to the snooker club with my grandad and it feels like we were just there. But, wait a minute, there's all this time in between.'(cxxxv)

An unreliable narrator, the rock star is finally given a name on the album's penultimate track. Mr Schwartz opens with Dear Prudence-style finger-plucked guitar, liberally enhanced by piano, woodblock, and subtle Bossa nova to create a dry, worn groove that Turner vocalises (an example of the mood affecting the lyrics and vocals). A sequel to a song that didn't make the cut, we find the titular character 'staying strong for the crew,' and 'having tea with the grips, asking after all the wives and the kids.'

It seems Mr Schwartz (a name inspired by a model of Alfa Romeo) is ruminating on the responsibilities of being the leader and the day-today coordination of leading a band, essentially being the MD of 'The Business', while at the same time 'smudging dubbin on your dancing shoes,' namely muddying the past with another meta-reference to Arctic Monkeys' history. Bringing things full circle, he muses on 'your little directorial debut,' reminding us of the video for the album's first single. It's an intimate, quiet song and is reflected in the live performances with Turner only in the spotlight. So slight it could be missed, but arguably the most informative song present.

The Car reaches its destination with Perfect Sense, the strings generating a vibe of completion or resolution, or simply an endpoint. Swirling in a manner akin to Brian Wilson, the song was created in a relatively short space of time, apparently arriving ready-made and the last to be written before the Butley Priory sessions. Although Matt Helders' drums sound annoyed, the band doesn't get too much of a look in with the focus on the lyrics, as our protagonist can conclude that 'Sometimes I wrap my head around it all and it makes perfect sense,' seemingly resolved to his fate.

Demonstrating Alex Turner's remarkable foresight, he observes; 'Keep reminding me that it ain't a race when my invincible streak turns onto the final straight,' which, given that their own streak (of number 1 albums) was about to fall at the feet of the mighty Taylor Swift, is disconcertingly accurate. The final line ('if that's what it takes to say goodnight,') caught the attention of many journalists who assumed that was a farewell from the band itself, a claim which they were all quick to deny.

Although he would claim that it was harder to draw definitive lines as to his inspirations, that's not the case here, which he confirmed to *Musikexpress:*

'In my earlier songs I described actual situations out of my life or the lives of my friends very concretely. But that phase is long gone, I haven't done that in forever. The characters and situations in these songs are fictitious. I am not trying to disguise autobiographical experiences as metaphors.'(cxxxvii)

The Car is an exquisitely tailored, mature piece of work, and is considerably more accessible than its predecessor. The lyrical approach of less-is-more suits the space that the strings provide, in contrast to the sometimes-cluttered style of what went before. The mellifluous instruments add a sense of scale, being ambitious and full of textures and innovation, while the pure musicianship is delivered by a group of young men completely comfortable with themselves and their abilities. As always, they followed their instinct. Where *Tranquility Base Hotel + Casino* was an experiment or a challenge Turner set himself, here everything feels more natural and a result of the band truly collaborating.

For this writer, *The Car* represents the journey to get to this point, and while travelling one's mind wanders. Ideas and thoughts pop into the head and exit equally abruptly and, now that Turner is approaching his fifth decade, nostalgia or reminiscence is simply unavoidable; his memory is starting to leak, as they do when we reach a certain point in life. At points, it can feel like the band is fighting with the tempo of the songs, but the strings eventually win out, generating imagery and mood that's additional to the lyrics. Back when recording *AM,* they discovered the joys of the studio rather than viewing it as a necessity, and *The Car* is perhaps the best summation of that process to date.

Confident, still observant but slightly resigned, Turner's voice is more malleable than before while he and Cook unleash some fresh ideas on the guitar. As before, it's not clear who plays what, but we do know that Matt Helders responds to the challenge of slower-tempo music well, as he told *Spin:* 'Now I appreciate restraint and being able to play a groove in a really good way. It's not any less fun for me, contrary to what it might look like. Even though the drumming is calm and more laid back, it's as much fun as it is to play more showy.'(cxxxix)

The reviews for *The Car* were positive. *NME* called the group 'the last – and greatest – band of their generation still operating at the highest level,'(cxl) while *Rolling Stone* declared it 'one of their most accomplished and impressive records so far.'(cxli) Elsewhere, *The Independent* said the songs were 'designed to reward deep listening, (and) they mark, arguably, the start of the post-song era, where form and structure give way to mood and imagery.'(cxlii)

Although I Ain't Quite Where I Think I Am hit number 23 in the UK Singles Chart in the same week (two places above There'd Better Be a Mirrorball), there was no way *The Car* could compete with Taylor Swift. Despite shifting 119,016 units, it failed to take the top spot in the UK Album Charts, the first time in their career they had failed to do so. *AM* also returned to the top 10 in the same week, but even the combined sales of the two albums couldn't come close to *Midnights* which, as well as shifting 204,000 units, broke a string of sales, streaming, digital, vinyl, and official chart records globally, including the most-streamed album in one day on Spotify. The streak was finally over.

UK Album Chart – Top 10 – 28th October 2022:

1. *Midnights* – Taylor Swift
2. ***The Car* – Arctic Monkeys**
3. *Hugo* – Loyle Carner
4. *Direction Of the Heart* – Simple Minds
5. *Impossible Princess* – Kylie Minogue
6. = – Ed Sheeran
7. *Being Funny in A Foreign Language* – The 1975
8. *Harry's House* – Harry Styles
9. *The Highlights* – Weeknd
10. ***AM* – Arctic Monkeys**

Alas, it makes for a downbeat ending, but we can be reassured that, if records mean a lot to fans, they mean little to the band, who continue to be one of the most important and best groups in the world. As their sales (both ticket and album) performance proves, their popularity is undimmed and indeed, the immediate future looks bright, with a mammoth worldwide tour and possible Glastonbury headline slot in 2023.

As has been the case throughout their career, where they go after that is entirely up to them, and as one of the most successful, innovative bands in the history of rock music they have earnt that right. Truly, one of the all-time greats.

Shame about the name though.

THE END

References

(i) https://pitchfork.com/features/5-10-15-20/8832-alex-turner/
(ii) https://pitchfork.com/features/5-10-15-20/8832-alex-turner/
(iii) https://pitchfork.com/features/5-10-15-20/8832-alex-turner/
(iv) https://pitchfork.com/features/5-10-15-20/8832-alex-turner/
(v) http://www.hour.ca/music/music.aspx?iIDArticle=8612
(vi) https://www.theguardian.com/music/2005/sep/30/popandrock.arcticmonkeys
(vii) http://www.prefixmag.com/features/arctic-monkeys/arent-fooling-around-part-1-of-2/12565/
(viii) BBC - South Yorkshire - Entertainment - Too much Monkey business?
(ix) https://www.theguardian.com/music/2005/jul/28/popandrock.arcticmonkeys
(x) Arctic Monkeys : Birmingam Carling Bar Academy, Sunday August 14 (nme.com)
(xi) Arctic Monkeys | Culture | The Guardian
(xii) https://www.theguardian.com/music/2005/sep/30/popandrock.arcticmonkeys
(xiii) Arctic Monkeys diss 'annoying' Kaiser Chiefs (nme.com)
(xiv) https://www.nme.com/reviews/reviews-arctic-monkeys-7837-317720
(xv) https://www.rollingstone.com/music/music-album-reviews/whatever-people-say-i-am-thats-what-im-not-201301/
(xvi) https://www.theguardian.com/music/2006/jan/13/popandrock.shopping6
(xvii) https://pitchfork.com/reviews/albums/497-whatever-people-say-i-am-thats-what-im-not/
(xviii) https://www.irishtimes.com/culture/year-of-the-monkeys-1.1013781
(xix) https://www.nme.com/news/music/arctic-monkeys-605-1355037
(xx) https://www.nme.com/news/music/arctic-monkeys-571-1364412
(xxi) https://www.nme.com/reviews/reviews-arctic-monkeys-7905-310345
(xxii) https://drownedinsound.com/releases/7382/reviews/791215-arctic-monkeys-who-the-fuck-are-arctic-monkeys
(xxiii) https://www.nme.com/news/music/arctic-monkeys-634-1361647
(xxiv) https://www.nme.com/news/music/arctic-monkeys-582-1366157

(xxv) https://www.nme.com/news/music/arctic-monkeys-537-1358102
(xxvi) https://www.nme.com/news/music/arctic-monkeys-509-1355283
(xxvii) https://www.nme.com/news/music/arctic-monkeys-485-1351710
(xxviii) https://www.nme.com/news/music/arctic-monkeys-566-1346336
(xxix) https://www.nme.com/reviews/reviews-arctic-monkeys-8323-333641
(xxx) https://www.nme.com/blogs/nme-blogs/arctic-monkeys-nme-interview-2007-favourite-worst-nightmare-2307701
(xxxi) https://www.nme.com/reviews/reviews-arctic-monkeys-8427-332366
(xxxii) https://www.theguardian.com/music/2007/apr/20/popandrock.alexispetridis
(xxxiii) https://pitchfork.com/reviews/albums/10150-favourite-worst-nightmare/
(xxxiv) https://www.nme.com/news/music/arctic-monkeys-653-1398470
(xxxv) https://www.nme.com/news/music/arctic-monkeys-649-1397834
(xxxvi) https://www.nme.com/news/music/arctic-monkeys-644-1396617
(xxxvii) https://www.nme.com/photos/arctic-monkeys-alex-turner-ivor-novellos-2007-2077517
(xxxviii) https://www.nme.com/news/music/arctic-monkeys-427-1325341
(xxxix) https://www.nme.com/news/music/the-last-shadow-puppets-63-1326872
(xl) https://www.nme.com/news/music/the-last-shadow-puppets-58-1322460
(xli) https://www.nme.com/news/music/arctic-monkeys-437-1329871
(xlii) https://www.nme.com/news/music/arctic-monkeys-367-1320508
(xliii) https://www.nme.com/news/music/arctic-monkeys-384-1309549
(xliv) https://www.nme.com/blogs/nme-blogs/arctic-monkeys-humbug-2009-interview-2310970
(xlv) https://www.theguardian.com/music/2009/aug/20/arctic-monkeys-humbug-cd-review
(xlvi) https://pitchfork.com/reviews/albums/13374-humbug/
(xlvii) https://www.nme.com/reviews/reviews-arctic-monkeys-10775-321646
(xlviii) https://www.nme.com/news/music/arctic-monkeys-211-1293695

(xlix) https://www.rocksbackpages.com/Library/Article/alex-turner-tupacs-california-love-is-my-karaoke-tune-of-choice

(l) https://www.rocksbackpages.com/Library/Article/alex-turner-tupacs-california-love-is-my-karaoke-tune-of-choice

(li) https://www.nme.com/news/music/arctic-monkeys-328-1294065

(lii) https://www.nme.com/news/music/arctic-monkeys-303-1302092

(liii) https://www.nme.com/news/music/arctic-monkeys-265-1296505

(liv) https://www.soundonsound.com/people/james-ford-producing-arctic-monkeys?amp

(lv) https://www.theguardian.com/music/2011/may/27/alex-turner-arctic-monkeys-interview

(lvi) https://www.nme.com/news/music/arctic-monkeys-235-1285862

(lvii) https://www.nme.com/reviews/reviews-arctic-monkeys-12113-305625

(lviii) https://thequietus.com/articles/06438-arctic-monkeys-suck-it-and-see-review#:~:text=So%20it's%20a%20little%20startling,clever%20couplets%20still%20evident%20throughout.

(lix) https://www.theguardian.com/music/2011/jun/02/arctic-monkeys-suck-it-and-see-review

(lx) https://pitchfork.com/reviews/albums/15450-suck-it-and-see/

(lxi) https://www.spin.com/2011/06/arctic-monkeys-graduates/

(lxii) https://www.nme.com/news/music/arctic-monkeys-304-1275020

(lxiii) https://www.shortlist.com/news/arctic-monkeys#image-rotator-1

(lxiv) https://www.nme.com/news/music/arctic-monkeys-281-1273649

(lxv) https://www.nme.com/news/music/arctic-monkeys-275-1269034

(lxvi) https://www.nme.com/news/music/arctic-monkeys-277-1279825

(lxvii) https://www.gq.com/story/alex-turner-gq-music-issue

(lxviii) https://www.nme.com/news/music/arctic-monkeys-231-1284447

(lxix) https://www.nme.com/news/music/arctic-monkeys-213-1277152

(lxx) https://www.nme.com/news/music/arctic-monkeys-205-1271459

(lxxi) https://www.nme.com/news/music/arctic-monkeys-200-1283350

(lxxii) https://www.nme.com/news/music/arctic-monkeys-210-1273195

(lxxiii) https://www.nme.com/news/music/arctic-monkeys-204-1270320

(lxxiv) https://www.nme.com/news/music/arctic-monkeys-199-1271809

(lxxv) https://www.nme.com/news/music/arctic-monkeys-162-1252844

(lxxvi) https://www.nme.com/news/music/arctic-monkeys-191-1260629

(lxxvii) https://www.nme.com/news/music/arctic-monkeys-185-1260948

(lxxviii) https://www.nme.com/news/music/arctic-monkeys-180-1267525

(lxxix) https://www.nme.com/news/music/arctic-monkeys-177-1266181

(lxxx) https://www.nme.com/news/music/arctic-monkeys-172-1264384

(lxxxi) https://www.nme.com/news/music/arctic-monkeys-186-1263201

(lxxxii) https://www.nme.com/news/music/arctic-monkeys-171-1264151

(lxxxiii) https://www.nme.com/news/music/arctic-monkeys-160-1252025

(lxxxiv) https://www.nme.com/news/music/arctic-monkeys-178-1266582

(lxxxv) https://www.nme.com/news/music/arctic-monkeys-165-1259546

(lxxxvi) https://www.nme.com/news/music/arctic-monkeys-157-1250311

(lxxxvii) https://www.nme.com/news/music/arctic-monkeys-178-1266582

(lxxxviii) https://www.nme.com/reviews/reviews-arctic-monkeys-14752-322783

(lxxxix) https://www.theguardian.com/music/2013/sep/08/arctic-monkeys-am-review#:~:text=But%20while%20AM%20isn't,satisfying%20album%20since%20their%20debut.

(xc) https://www.timeout.com/music/arctic-monkeys-am-album-review

(xci) https://www.theguardian.com/music/2013/oct/27/arctic-monkeys-mexico-beatlemania

(xcii) https://www.nme.com/news/music/arctic-monkeys-145-1257414

(xciii) https://www.nme.com/news/music/arctic-monkeys-105-1245384

(xciv) https://www.nme.com/news/music/arctic-monkeys-94-1230768

(xcv) https://www.nme.com/news/music/arctic-monkeys-78-1234691
(xcvi) https://www.nme.com/news/music/arctic-monkeys-7-1193452
(xcvii) https://www.nme.com/news/music/arctic-monkeys-71-1229165
(xcviii) https://www.nme.com/news/music/arctic-monkeys-59-1238914
(xcix) https://www.nme.com/news/music/arctic-monkeys-51-1230691
(c) https://www.nme.com/news/music/arctic-monkeys-49-1241318
(ci) https://www.nme.com/news/music/arctic-monkeys-85-1240959
(cii) https://www.nme.com/news/music/arctic-monkeys-41-1241437
(ciii) https://www.nme.com/news/music/the-last-shadow-puppets-34-1192223
(civ) https://www.nme.com/features/the-last-shadow-puppets-the-full-nme-cover-interview-757016
(cv) https://www.nme.com/news/music/the-last-shadow-puppets-16-1196115
(cvi) https://www.billboard.com/music/rock/inside-arctic-monkeys-tranquility-base-hotel-casino-alex-turner-interview-8357304/
(cvii) https://www.rollingstone.com/music/music-features/arctic-monkeys-start-over-628863/
(cviii) https://www.nme.com/news/music/arctic-monkeys-discuss-lyrics-departure-sound-autobiographical-new-album-2300317
(cix) https://www.musicweek.com/publishing/read/alex-turner-has-written-another-masterpiece-sony-atv-s-guy-moot-on-arctic-monkeys-amazing-comeback/072234
(cx) https://www.nme.com/news/music/alex-turner-explains-tranquility-base-hotel-casino-didnt-end-solo-album-2306713
(cxi) https://www.nme.com/reviews/arctic-monkeys-tranquility-base-hotel-casino-review-2306655
(cxii) https://pitchfork.com/reviews/albums/arctic-monkeys-tranquility-base-hotel-and-casino/
(cxiii) https://www.theguardian.com/music/2018/may/13/arctic-monkeys-tranquility-base-hotel-obsever-review
(cxiv) https://www.nme.com/news/music/alex-turner-arctic-monkeys-interview-band-rather-than-solo-2320874
(cxv) https://www.billboard.com/music/rock/inside-arctic-monkeys-tranquility-base-hotel-casino-alex-turner-interview-8357304/
(cxvi) https://www.rollingstone.com/music/music-features/arctic-monkeys-start-over-628863/

(cxvii) https://www.nme.com/news/music/arctic-monkeys-alex-turner-speaks-politics-music-past-tax-controversy-2321805
(cxviii) https://www.nme.com/news/music/arctic-monkeys-open-up-on-the-polarising-reaction-to-their-new-album-and-their-plans-for-a-follow-up-2364063
(cxix) https://www.nme.com/news/music/arctic-monkeys-alex-turner-making-music-in-40-years-2368027
(cxx) https://www.nme.com/news/music/feels-like-cover-arctic-monkeys-2386100
(cxxi) https://www.nme.com/news/music/arctic-monkeys-drummer-matt-helders-working-solo-album-2387984
(cxxii) https://www.nme.com/news/music/former-arctic-monkeys-bassist-andy-nicholson-tells-us-about-life-after-the-band-and-going-solo-as-goldteeth-2508404
(cxxiii) https://musicfeeds.com.au/features/the-arctic-monkeys-matt-helders-on-why-we-wont-be-waiting-another-five-years-for-a-new-album/#/slide/1
(cxxiv) https://www.nme.com/news/music/sheffields-leadmill-react-to-arctic-monkeys-raffle-raising-100000-to-them-its-a-guitar-to-us-its-a-lifeline-2736373
(cxxv) https://musicfeeds.com.au/features/alexandra-savior-on-songwriting-working-with-alex-turner-visting-australia/
(cxxvi) https://www.musicweek.com/talent/read/ian-mcandrew-talks-arctic-monkeys-live-album-lockdown-and-new-music/082167
(cxxvii) https://www.bigissue.com/culture/music/exclusive-7-things-alex-turner-revealed-to-us-about-new-arctic-monkeys-album-the-car/
(cxxviii) https://www.nme.com/news/music/new-arctic-monkeys-album-is-pretty-much-finished-and-coming-in-2022-says-matt-helders-3093991
(cxxix) https://www.nme.com/news/music/matt-helders-on-arctic-monkeys-new-album-its-never-gonna-be-like-r-u-mine-and-all-that-stuff-again-3226299
(cxxx) https://www.bigissue.com/culture/music/arctic-monkeys-the-car-alex-turner-martin-compston/
(cxxxi) https://www.theguardian.com/music/2022/sep/30/arctic-monkeys-alex-turner-im-comfortable-with-the-idea-that-things-dont-have-to-be-a-pop-song
(cxxxii) https://www.theguardian.com/music/2022/sep/30/arctic-monkeys-alex-turner-im-comfortable-with-the-idea-that-things-dont-have-to-be-a-pop-song
(cxxxiii) https://www.theguardian.com/music/2022/sep/30/arctic-monkeys-alex-turner-im-comfortable-with-the-idea-that-things-dont-have-to-be-a-pop-song

(cxxxiv) https://www.theguardian.com/music/2022/sep/30/arctic-monkeys-alex-turner-im-comfortable-with-the-idea-that-things-dont-have-to-be-a-pop-song

(cxxxv) https://www.bigissue.com/culture/music/exclusive-7-things-alex-turner-revealed-to-us-about-new-arctic-monkeys-album-the-car/

(cxxxvi) https://docs.google.com/document/d/15VcdscnfsAK4nUJXrImlzsTMw_k7lb0nUPLd017shnY/mobilebasic

(cxxxvii) https://docs.google.com/document/d/15VcdscnfsAK4nUJXrImlzsTMw_k7lb0nUPLd017shnY/mobilebasic

(cxxxviii) https://www.nme.com/big-reads/arctic-monkeys-cover-interview-2022-the-car-3332436

(cxxxix) https://www.spin.com/featured/arctic-monkeys-the-car-cover-story/

(cxl) https://www.nme.com/reviews/album/arctic-monkeys-the-car-review-3330197

(cxli) https://www.rollingstone.co.uk/music/album-reviews/arctic-monkeys-the-car-review-24068/

(cxlii) https://www.independent.co.uk/arts-entertainment/music/reviews/arctic-monkeys-album-review-the-car-b2207734.html

ABOUT THE AUTHOR

Richard Bowes writes about music as much as he can, regularly reviewing albums and gigs and conducting interviews for Live4ever.com and Gigwise.

'Modern Music Masters – Arctic Monkeys' is his third book. 'Some Might Say – The Definitive Story of Oasis' was published in 2020, followed by 'Modern Music Masters – The Verve' in 2021.

For more information about the Modern Music Masters series:
modernmusicmastersuk@gmail.com
www.modernmusicmasters.uk